The Age of Vasari

**A Loan Exhibition
Under the High Patronage
Of His Excellency, Egidio Ortona
The Ambassador of Italy
To the United States**

**Art Gallery
University of Notre Dame, Notre Dame, Indiana
February 22 - March 31, 1970**

**University Art Gallery
State University of New York at Binghamton
April 12 - May 10, 1970**

Foreword

In the spring of 1966 Professor Federico Zeri attributed a small panel in the University of Notre Dame Collection to Giorgio Vasari. This attribution was the starting point for Dean Porter, Curator of the Art Gallery at Notre Dame, to plan the present exhibition. The University Art Gallery of the State University of New York at Binghamton joined this project and we are all indebted to Mr. Porter for his initiative work and enthusiasm in this undertaking.

We express our sincere gratitude to His Excellency, Egidio Ortona, Italian Ambassador to the United States, for accepting the patronage of this exhibition.

To Miss Mary M. Davis and the Samuel H. Kress Foundation we are grateful for their unfailing support. Miss Davis was instrumental in assisting us with several important loans, and the catalogue could not have been possible without the generous financial support of the Kress Foundation.

Many individuals and institutions were involved in the process of assembling this exhibition and our gratitude is expressed to all of them on the following pages of this catalogue.

Finally, the generous support of our Administrations has enabled us to bring this undertaking to a successful end.

Rev. Anthony J. Lauck, Director
Art Gallery, University of Notre Dame

Michael Milkovich, Director
University Art Gallery
State University of New York at Binghamton

Introduction

Few of the "Old Masters" are better qualified to be the focal point of an exhibition in a university than is Giorgio Vasari. In an age when the university stresses the need for the liberal and the fine arts, history, theology and sociology, Vasari is the ideal individual. The versatility of Vasari has been criticized as well as applauded. As a painter, historians have sacrificed him to the lower ranks. As a draughtsman he has faired somewhat better but still is in the shadows of his Florentine contemporaries. However, as an art historian, few scholars working on the Quattrocento and the Cinquecento have been able to overlook Vasari's *Le Vite de'Piu Eccellenti Pittori, Scultori e Architettori Italiani*. Scholarship demands primary source material. Vasari provides the art historian with contemporary information on the artists, their works and the dates of the execution of these pieces. His information is not only straightforward and factual, but also his anecdotes regarding the personality of an artist provide the reader with intimate details of the artist's life, habits and pecularities. In his *Vite* Vasari also introduces the reader to art historical theory with his notion of *progress*. Vasari's knowledge and interest in classical antiquity is evident in his writings as well as his paintings and drawings. His theory of style, illuminated in Maurice Poirier's discussion of *disegno* in this catalogue, has long been of a controversial nature to the aesthetician, and is one of the first, if not the first basis for conceptual art. Nor can we overlook Vasari the collector. His *Libro dei Disegni*, assembled to illustrate his *Vite*, is the first of the great collections. Vasari's relationships to the political figures, the Medici, to literary personages such as Vincenzo Borghini, Pietro Aretino and Benedetto Varchi, as well as his affiliations with the Papacy, also provide us with a penetrating insight into sixteenth century Italy. All of his activities are well documented by his *Vite* as well as by the volumes of letters that are available for our perusal.

Vasari was a figure of great immediacy. His travels brought him into contact with virtually all of the noteworthy artists of this period. He apprenticed under Andrea del Sarto and Baccio Bandinelli, became a close friend of Michelangelo, was a companion of Francesco Salviati, and his travels brought him into contact with Romano and Titian.

He organized some of the most significant projects in the history of Florentine art. Few artists have attempted so much and met with as great success as Vasari. In 1536, given the task of preparing the decorations for the reception of Emperor Charles V in Florence, Vasari distributed the work to Giovanni Corsi, Luigi Guicciardini, Palla Rucellai, Alessandro Corsini, and Niccolò Tribolo. While in Venice in 1542 he created the decorations for Pietro Aretino's *La Talanta*. In 1562 Vasari was instrumental in the foundation of the Florentine Academy, the *Accademia del Disegno*. In 1564, Vasari, along with Agnolo Bronzino, Benvenuto Cellini, and Bartolommeo Ammannati, was charged by the *Accademia* to prepare the funeral ceremony for the first lieutenant and head of their *Accademia*, Michelangelo. Vasari in 1565, with Vincenzo Borghini, was placed in charge of the decoration of Florence for the marriage of Francesco de'Medici and Giovanna of Austria. While Vasari was performing these various artistic services, he was also involved with one of the most ambitious projects recorded in Florentine history: the decoration of the Palazzo Vecchio. From 1555 to 1572, Vasari was to remain the "master supervisor" of this enormous project. Approximately thirty artists, if we include the *Studiolo di Francesco I*, worked on the decoration of this grand structure. During the last three years of Vasari's life, the artist was to work on the decoration of Brunelleschi's cupola for Santa Maria del Fiore, the Dome of the Florence Cathedral.

Even if we are to question Vasari for his lack of ability as a painter, we must only do so in light of his other achievements. Few have accomplished as much . . . few have exerted as great an influence as Vasari. Artistically, he created a style that was followed by Giovanni Battista Naldini, Cristofano Gherardi, Jan van der Straeten (Stradano), Francesco Morandini, Prospero Fontana, Jacopo Zucchi, Marco da Faenza, and Carlo Portelli, to mention a few. This, however, is not Vasari's most significant contribution; in fact history will overlook this role of Vasari more often than not. Art historians will, however, remember Vasari's accounts of the Sack of Rome, they will reacquaint themselves through his writings with the acid personality of Baccio Bandinelli and the sickness of Jacopo Pontormo. They will recall the glory that was Italy . . . they will relive the tumultuous period of the Catholic Reformation . . . all of this through the eyes of Giorgio Vasari.

Michael Milkovich
Dean A. Porter

Acknowledgments

This exhibition could not have been possible without the enthusiastic support of collectors, dealers, university and municipal museums in this country and Canada. Our requests, except in the cases where the loan was thought to be a great risk, were considered generously and we are grateful for this confidence.

We are indebted to all who contributed to the catalogue either as a scholar or as a patron. Dr. Irving Zupnick, Professor of Art History at the State University of New York at Binghamton, contributes with his brilliant essay on the 16th century style. To Mr. Maurice Poirier from the Institute of Fine Arts, New York University and a Fellow of the Samuel H. Kress Foundation, we are grateful for permitting us to publish his recent work on *disegno;* also our gratitude is extended to Mr.-Richard-Raymond Alasko who wrote the essay and catalogue notes for the medallions and has helped in designing the catalogue and the exhibition installation at Notre Dame.

In the advisory capacity there were several who have been most generous with their time and assistance. Mr. Janos Scholz with his enthusiastic support as a collector, a connoisseur, and as a friend, must receive special commendation. Without his words of encouragement the exhibition would never have materialized. Miss Felice Stampfle, Curator of Drawings at the Pierpont Morgan Library and Mr. Jacob Bean, Curator of Drawings at The Metropolitan Museum of Art were extremely helpful in our selection of the drawings. Mr. Edmund Pillsbury of Harvard University made several suggestions on the paintings as well as the drawings, recommending objects that would enhance the exhibition.

We gratefully acknowledge the assistance and support received by our colleagues and friends: Dr. Alessandro Contini-Bonacossi, Mr. Charles H. Sawyer, Mr. Henry Hope, Mr. Perry T. Rathbone, Miss Agnes Mongan, Mr. John Maxon, Mr. Harold Joachim, Mr. Alfred J. Jakstas, Mr. John R. Craft, Mr. Willis F. Woods, Dr. Bob Jones, Jr., Mr. Peter O. Marlow, Mr. Philippe de Montebello, Mr. Carl J. Weinhardt, Mr. Robert L. Manning, Mr. William Osmun, Mr. Anthony M. Clark, Mr. Nicholas M. Acquavella, Mr. William Mayglothling, Mr. Michael Hall, Mr. W. E. Mills, Mr. Harry H. Sperling, Mr. William Voelkle, Miss Alice Tully, Miss Jean Sutherland Boggs, Dr. Evan H. Turner, Mr. Pinkney Near, Mr. Phillip J. Carlson, Mr. Curtis G. Coley, Mr. Richard E. Fuller, Mr. Otto Wittmann, Mr. Donald G. Humphrey, Mr. W. H. Janson, Mr. Thomas J. McCormick, Mrs. Elaine Dee, and Miss Lucy Gabriel.

We are always indebted to those who work on many aspects of the exhibition and its installation. Special mention is due to Mr. Frederick Geissel, Preparator at the University of Notre Dame and Mr. Walter Luckert, Gallery Technician at the University Art Gallery in Binghamton, who with great skill worked on the installation of the exhibition. Miss Elizabeth Van Horn, Assistant Curator of the University Art Gallery, has been of great help in the various aspects of this show. To our secretaries, Mrs. Norma Denby and Mrs. Martha McKenzie, go our hearty thanks. And finally to those students, particularly to Miss Marilyn Reed, Mr. John Anderson, Mr. Thomas Bower, Mr. Stephen Spiro, Miss Sharon Loganzo and Mr. Steven Rosen, who at the University of Notre Dame and the State University of New York at Binghamton, have contributed so much of their time with the exhibition, is due our praise.

M.M.
D.P.

Lenders to the Exhibition

Museum of Art, University of Michigan, Ann Arbor, Michigan
Museum of Art, Indiana University, Bloomington, Indiana
Museum of Fine Arts, Boston, Massachusetts
The Fogg Art Museum, Harvard University, Cambridge, Massachusetts
Ackland Memorial Art Center, University of North Carolina, Chapel Hill, North
      Carolina
The Art Institute of Chicago, Chicago, Illinois
Columbia Museum of Art, Columbia, South Carolina
The Detroit Institute of Arts, Detroit, Michigan
Bob Jones University, Greenville, South Carolina
The Wadsworth Atheneum, Hartford, Connecticut
Museum of Fine Arts of Houston, Houston, Texas
The John Herron Art Museum, Indianapolis, Indiana
Lessing Rosenwald Collection, Alverthorpe Gallery, Jenkintown, Pennsylvania
Mr. and Mrs. Robert L. Manning, Kew Gardens, New York
Los Angeles County Museum of Art, Los Angeles, California
The Minneapolis Institute of Arts, Minneapolis, Minnesota
Acquavella Galleries Inc., New York City
Mr. Walter P. Chrysler, Jr., New York City
The Cooper-Hewitt Museum of Decorative Arts and Design
      Smithsonian Institution, New York City
Mr. Michael Hall, New York City
Michael Hall Fine Arts Inc., New York City
Mr. and Mrs. Julius S. Held, New York City
Mr. and Mrs. Jacob M. Kaplan, New York City
F. Kleinberger & Co., Inc., New York City
Mr. Jack Linsky, New York City
The Metropolitan Museum of Art, New York City
Pierpont Morgan Library, New York City
Mr. Norbert Roesler, New York City
Mr. and Mrs. Janos Scholz, New York City
Mr. Victor D. Spark, New York City
Miss Alice Tully, New York City
Mr. Ian Woodner, New York City
Anonymous Loans, New York City
Art Gallery, University of Notre Dame, Notre Dame, Indiana
National Gallery of Canada, Ottawa, Canada
The Philadelphia Museum of Art, Philadelphia, Pennsylvania
Virginia Museum of Fine Arts, Richmond, Virginia
Mr. Milton Hebald, Rome, Italy
Achenbach Foundation for Graphic Arts, California Palace of the Legion of Honor
      San Francisco, California
M. H. de Young Memorial Museum, San Francisco, California
John and Mable Ringling Museum of Art, Sarasota, Florida
Seattle Art Museum, Seattle, Washington
The Toledo Museum of Art, Toledo, Ohio
Philbrook Art Center, Tulsa, Oklahoma
The Library of Congress, Rosenwald Collection, Washington, District of Columbia
The National Gallery of Art, Washington, District of Columbia
Mr. Edmund Pillsbury, Washington, District of Columbia

Speculations Concerning Mannerism

The realistic High Renaissance style, as it was practiced by Raphael in the Vatican *stanze* early in the sixteenth century, creates an optical illusion of reality which is successful to the degree that it imitates visual experience and raises it to a higher level of significance. The relatively abstract style we call *Mannerism*, that was practiced throughout most of the sixteenth century, obeyed inner impulses, unique in some cases to particular artists, and was directed at a sophisticated audience that was ready to view it in its own terms. As this stylistic tendency fell from fashion's grace at the end of the sixteenth century, yielding its place to a new wave of realism and a new concept of artistic relevance, it was attacked by Giovanni Bellori, for example, for its abuse of artistic license, and for the next two hundred years and more the works created in accordance with its highly personal and esoteric aesthetic remained in relative obscurity. It is only during the past forty years really that the Mannerists have returned to respectability, and that art historians have been interested enough to search for positive values in their art. The reason may be that Mannerism is something of a bastard style, mingling figurative realities and abstractive principles to create a composite effect, which does not always produce successful offspring. Nevertheless, Mannerism is interesting both for its artistic creations and for what it reveals as an historical phenomenon. Its body of aesthetic principles shows little sense of organization and much vagueness, and therefore only indirectly explains what transpired in the act of creation; but this is to be expected of a movement in which intuition replaced rules, and accuracy of imitation is no longer the measure of success.

Vasari seems not to have understood the nature of the Mannerist's contribution to the greater historical movement launched in the early Renaissance, and he lacked the acumen and the critical vocabulary to define it as more than a search for the nebulous quality that he called "grace." Even early in the present century, Mannerism found no place in Heinrich Wolfflin's system, whereby he sought to link the Renaissance to the Baroque as part of a "natural" development cycle, since there is no way to consider it as a transitional phase between these two essentially realistic developments. But if we keep our historical perspective unclouded by *a priori* theories of progress and cycles, it becomes clear that the so-called Manneristic Style between circa 1520 and circa 1590 is an example of a recurrent tendency that surfaced twice before in the Italian Renaissance; once in the second half of the fourteenth, and once in the last quarter of the fifteen century. In the earlier resurgence it came as a reaction against the realism of the Giottesque school continuing until it led to the style of the Papal Court at Avignon around 1400; and in the case of the later one, the stylizations of Pollaiuolo, Botticelli, and Verrocchio, from about 1475 on, are only separated from sixteenth century Mannerism by the relatively brief period that we know as the High Renaissance. Michelangelo, in fact, as a key figure in the creation of the Vatican style during the first decades of the sixteenth century, also can be seen as the most influential artist of Vasari's age, and as the most important pioneer in the creation of the Manneristic Style.

Mannerism, then, should be understood as a contrast to Realism, and, together with the latter, as one of the two major tendencies in conflict with one another throughout the Renaissance. Whereas realism seeks to *imitate* objective visual experience, mannerism *editorializes*, subordinating objectivity to subjective interpretation. The realist is interested in creating a tangible, experiental sensation of depth, surface, and texture. To this end, he minimizes the edges of forms and exploits the effects of light and shadow in order to create sensations that suggest palpable objects separated by intervening spaces. The mannerist, in contrast, is more concerned with treating his forms as reliefs in relationship on a plane. He is likely to emphasize the contours of figures and objects in order to provide a compositional "machinery" to create sensations of interrelationship and movement; such sensations being expressed in terms of continuity of line, through contacts, contiguities, and closures. The realist seeks to heighten expressiveness through the acting *performances* of the figures in his compositions, accurately rendered in terms of physiognomic reaction and gesture. Because of his realistic sense of logic and actuality, the postures and gestures of his figures are governed by his knowledge of the normative structure of man, and expressed as angular arrangements and foreshortened projections that reflect the ineluctable characteristics of the underlying skeletal matrix. The mannerist, in answer to an inner necessity, which was supported by the current Neo-Platonistic belief in cosmic unity, distorts physiognomy and gesture to meet compositional requirements that are germane to his art, even when they are not faithful to nature. In his works, the skeletal structure melts to conform to the linear flow of the relief on its plane, becoming malleable sometimes to the point of physical impossibility.

Michelangelo pointed the way in his early sculptured relief, the *Rape of Dejanira*, in which he fashioned a torrent of interwoven bodies into a spiraling garland around the central figure. He continually reinforced his contribution to the new style by creating figures, either painted or carved, that twisted in space, combining more than one side of the body in each axial view; so that each of the cardinal points would present the observer with a synthesis that summarized the dynamic interrelationship of the parts of the body. Later, Manneristic sculptors, like Giovanni da Bologna (fig. 1), were to sacrifice the elements of momentary synthesis to a unity of movement which suggests that the statues should be displayed on a turntable. Even in his late frescoes, the *Conversion of Saint Paul* (fig. 2), and the *Crucifixion of Saint Peter* (fig. 3) in the Cappella Paolina, which until quite recently were considered as evidence of his dotage, Michelangelo showed how figure compositions could be made to seem to whirl in spirals, or to suggest centrifugal and centripetal movements, as if they were subject to supernatural cosmic forces.

Allowing even for the powerful impetus given by Michelangelo, it is still surprising that an artistic development as successful as the High Renaissance was abandoned so quickly. The sudden change, beginning in Florence with Pontormo and Il Rosso, and even affecting Raphael, Giulio Romano, and their colleagues in Rome, before they had completed their Vatican projects, must mean that the stately harmonies of form, color, and space, exemplified by the *School of Athens* could no longer satisfy the artists' criteria for a work of art. As monumental and impressive as it was, the achievements of the realistic approach suddenly seemed bland. The grandeur of its spatial illusionism contributed to the weakening of the impact of the human drama; and the human drama, choreographed in classic balance under the influence of geometric order, already seems to lack fire in comparison with the work of Michelangelo. Although Michelangelo's influence was very important, we must look deeper to find the conceptual basis of Mannerism. Pontormo and Il Rosso began their innovations in Florence in his absence, tentatively and experimentally groping for their own solutions, and falling under

Fig. 1. *Rape of the Sabines*   GIOVANNI DA BOLOGNA
Loggia dei Lanzi, Florence   (Photo Alinari)

Fig. 2. *Conversion of Saint Paul*
Cappella Paolina, Rome

MICHELANGELO
(Photo Alinari)

Fig. 3. *Crucifixion of Saint Peter*
Cappella Paolina, Rome

MICHELANGELO
(Photo Alinari)

his influence only later on. Perhaps the most significant clue is that they shared a common origin with Michelangelo, working in Florence, which was the home of the Platonic Academy founded by the Medici and developed by the most important Neo-Platonist of the fifteenth century, Marsilio Ficino, who indelibly stamped his mark on sixteenth century aesthetics.

Mannerism was an attempt to sever art from the surface realities of life and to pursue it, not to a logical, but rather to an intuitive conclusion. Although we are far from certain about the origin of the term, *maniera,* it seems to have had a positive sense before it acquired a derogatory association in Bellori's usage. There is a clue to its meaning in *The Spiritual Espousals,* a theological treatise by Jan van Ruysbroeck, the influential fourteenth century mystic. Ruysbroeck asserts that the experience of a "delectable unity with God is as it were a darkness and *a lack of manner* and an incomprehensibility." He goes on to tell us that after such a mystic experience the recipient turns inward for essential rest, for none could endure a protracted revelation. During this period the intellect begins to examine and transform the overwhelming and ineffable experience, and in this process "recognition and comprehension consists in *manner* and *measure.*" Because man must communicate his experience both to himself and to others, he translates it into "many kinds of *images and manners.*" *Manner,* then, is the communicable form of the contemplative experience, and thus becomes a viable term for aesthetic theory.

Vasari can make little claim to being a philosopher, and thus for him *maniera* is a certain "grace exceeding measurement;" a nebulous stylistic quality which can be lost if the artist tries too hard to achieve it. In his usage the term seems to describe little more than an inherent personal sensitivity, which is manifest in style. But at its roots the concept that eluded Vasari belongs to the long lasting mystical tradition that links Ficino to Late Pagan and Early Christian philosophy. It relates to Plotinus' view that if the soul were made visible it would absorb the outward manifestation of the body within its aura. It is reminiscent of Augustine's concept of the cosmic "rhythm of relationships" of the "whole body inside and out," which would reveal to the soul, if it could be discerned, "so ravishing a beauty that no visible shapeliness of form that delights the eye—the mere minister of our mind—could be compared with it." This emphasis upon a form of experience unrelated to sensory data suggests a possibility for art that contrasts with the Renaissance's Aristotelian materialism as much as the views of Marsilio Ficino contrast with those of his contemporary Leonardo da Vinci, who was already too committed to his own principles to adopt new ones. Whereas Leonardo tells us that we can represent even man's soul "by the attitudes and movements of the limbs," Ficino foreshadows the Neo-Platonic aesthetics of the sixteenth century by completely severing the spiritual from the physical world, pointing out the meaninglessness and relativity of proportion, composition, and surface embellishments. Giordano Bruno was to further elucidate these ideas towards the end of the sixteenth century, asserting in terms which anticipate twentieth century phenomenology, that we must throw off the "corruptible accidents, the dimensions, the signs and figures, from that which lies under these things," if the intellect is to grasp the untrammeled essence of the things, themselves. Federigo Zuccaro belatedly published his *Idea dei scultori, pittori e architetti* in 1607, drawing this philosophical concept into the compass of aesthetics, particularly in his definition of *disegno interno.* By inward, or interior design, he means the concept which precedes the first sketch of a work of art. According to Zuccaro, "Design is neither matter nor body, nor the accident of any substance, but is the form, idea, rule, and object of the intellect in which the things comprehended are expressed." He tells us that "the goal of the external operation is a material thing, like the figure drawn or painted, etc. . . . the goal of the internal operation is an immaterial form representing the thing comprehended." With Zuccaro then, we arrive at the artistic equivalent of the mystic's experience, described over two centuries earlier by Ruysbroeck. *Disegno interno* is the process of translating the ineffable into the communicable.

And the ineffable, in the philosophy of all mystics from the beginnings of time, is the belief in the unity of all existence under Divine Power. The artist can communicate this essential verity by creating interrelationships that overcome the bland and misleading "facts" of sensory experience.

It may be that as you look at the works of art that reflect this philosophy you will not experience the sense of exaltation that you are supposed to feel. Aesthetic response can have something akin to mystic revelation; in the same way it requires a certain kind of sensitivity and a degree of faith. The same requirements would be necessary for the artists who seek to project such ideas. Not all of them, since most artists are followers rather than pioneers, have the same ability to strike the keynotes of a period; and an artistic movement as prolonged as this one was, is certain to suffer dilution. Nevertheless, if you are conscious of the difficulty of projecting a philosophy as intuitive and nebulous as Neo-Platonism, you will begin to appreciate Vasari's age as a historic period in which the assertion of artistic individuality broke down the tyranny of a highly integrated conceptual system, and, through this achievement, prepared the way for the new empiricism, and the dynamic inventiveness, of Baroque art, in the same way that the science and philosophy of the sixteenth century broke the spell of ancient and misleading authorities and opened the way to the modern era.

Irving L. Zupnick
State University of New York
Binghamton, New York

Paintings

P1. *Holy Family*   ANONYMOUS FLORENTINE

P6. *Madonna and Child*   JACOPO CARRUCCI, called IL PONTORMO

P10. *Portrait of a Lady*   FRANCESCO **MAZZOLA**, called **PARMIGIANINO**

P17. *Annunciation*   GIORGIO VASARI

P18 *The Temptation of St. Jerome*   GIORGIO VASARI

D39. *Ceiling Design for the Sala di Lorenzo il Magnifico*   GIORGIO VASARI

Florentine Painting in the Time of Vasari

The history of Florentine painting in the age of Vasari belongs chronologically to Mannerism, a style which Dr. Zupnick in the previous article, has discussed carefully. The span of Vasari's activity embraced the first two generations of Mannerists (from the 1540s to mid-1570s) a period which is all but a homogeneous one; it was the time in which many different elements indicated a certain revolt against the rationalism of the Renaissance.

The first generation of these artists was trained in the studios of the High Renaissance painters and the influences of Raphael, Andrea del Sarto, Correggio and the Venetians were evident in the first decades of the century; these trends can be seen in several works included in the present exhibition. In the more advanced stages there is a certain kind of perverse irrationality which became clear in the fundamental differences in the artist's concept: in the artificial landscape, the intensity of the motions and the distorted human figures.

The Holy Family (no. P1) by an anonymous painter shows the effect of Andrea del Sarto's style and at the same time we notice the irrational use of colors which in the work of Beccafumi (nos. P2, P3) also are evident with the distorted forms of human figures. The outstanding work by Nosadella is a work worthy of his master, Pellegrino Tibaldi, and clearly indicates the new approach.

In Pontormo we have a fully developed Mannerist, who brought to us the new elements with such fantasy and torment (nos. P5, P6). The artists represented in this exhibition to a greater or lesser degree project the general ideas of the period and form a unity to picture this restless artistic venture. Parmigianino (nos. P9, P10), Lelio Orsi (no. P12), Francesco Salviati (no. P14), Santi di Tito (no. P16), Francesco Morandini (no. P11), Scipione Pulzone (no. P13), and the painter of Flemish origin, Stradanus (no. P15) present us with the peculiarities of Mannerism, which have been discussed in this catalogue on several occasions.

The major protagonist of this undertaking, Giorgio Vasari, in the exhibited works from his early *Annunciation* (no. P17), *The Temptation of St. Jerome* (no. P18), to the *St. Mary Magdalen* (no. P19), *Holy Family* (no. P20) and *Abraham and Melchizedek* (no. P12) convincingly reflect the idea of his time, and his great achievements as an architect and biographer, deserves a period to be called the Age of Vasari.

Selected Bibliography

P. Barocchi, *Rosso Fiorentino,* Rome, 1950.
P. Barocchi, *Complementi al Vasari Pittore,* Atti dell'Accademia Toscana-di Scienze
    e Lettere, Florence, 1963-1964, pp. 253-309.
P. Barocchi, *Vasari Pittore*, Milan, 1964.
L. Becherucci, *Manieristi Toscani*, Bergamo, 2nd ed., 1949.
Between Renaissance and Baroque, exhibition catalogue, City Art Gallery, Manchester, 1965.

A. Blunt, *Artistic Theory in Italy 1400-1600*, London, 1940.

G. Briganti, *La Maniera Italiana*, Erfurt, 1961.

W. R. Carden, *The Life of Giorgio Vasari. A study of the Later Renaissance in Italy*, London, 1910.

A. Chastel, *The Crisis of the Renaissance*, Skira, Geneva, 1968.

F. M. Clapp, *Jacopo Carucci da Pontormo, His Life and Work*, New Haven, 1916.

B. F. Davidson, "Vasari's Deposition in Arezzo", *The Art Bulletin*, XXXVI, Sept. 1954, pp. 228-231.

A. Emiliani, *Il Bronzino*, Milan, 1960.

S. Freedberg. *Parmigianino, His Works in Painting*, Cambridge, Mass., 1950.

W. F. Friedlaender, *Mannerism and Anti-Mannerism in Italian Painting*, Columbia University Press, 1957.

C. Gould, *An Introduction to Italian Renaissance Painting*, Phaidon Press, London, 1957.

F. Hartt, *Giulio Romano*, New Haven, 1958.

F. Hartt, *History of Italian Renaissance Art*, Abrams, New York, 1969.

D. Hay, ed., *The Age of the Renaissance*, London, 1967.

J. Judey, *Domenico Beccafumi*, Freiburg, 1932.

R. Klein & H. Zerner, *Italian Art, 1500-1600*, Sources and Documents in the History of Art, Prentice-Hall, 1966.

A. K. McComb, *Agnolo Bronzino, His Life and Works*, Cambridge, 1928.

Mostra del Cinquecento Toscano, Firenze, 1940.

Mostra di Lelio Orsi, Reggio Emilia, 1950.

Mostra del Pontormo e del Primo Manierismo Fiorentino, Firenze, 1956.

Pontormo to Greco—The Age of Mannerism, Herron Art Museum, Indianapolis, 1954.

E. Toesca, *Il Pontormo*, Rome, 1943.

De Triomf van het Manierisme, exhibition catalogue, Rijksmuseum, Amsterdam, 1955.

G. Vasari, *Lives of the Most Eminent Painters, Sculptors and Architects*, trans. by G. du C. De Vere, 10 vols., Medici Society, London, 1912-15.

A. Venturi, *Storia Dell'Arte Italiana—La Pitura del Cinquecento*, Vol. IX, 1-7, Milan, 1924-34.

L. Venturi, *The Sixteenth Century*, Skira, 1956.

H. Voss, *Die Malerei der Spätrenaissance in Rom und Florenz*, Berlin, 1920, 2 vols.

F. Wuertenberger, *Mannerism*, Vienna, 1963 (with extensive bibliography).

I. L. Zupnick, "The *Aesthetics* of the Early Mannerists," *Art Bulletin*, XXV (1953), pp. 302-306.

I. L. Zupnick, "The Iconology of Style (or Woelfflin Reconsidered)," *Journal of Aesthetics and Art Criticism*, XIX (1961), pp. 263-273.

I. L. Zupnick, "Pontormo's Early Style," *Art Bulletin*, 1965, pp. 344-353.

ANONYMOUS FLORENTINE
16th Century

P1. *Holy Family*

Oil on panel, 47 1/4 x 33 7/8 inches
Lent by H. Kleinberger & Co., Inc.
Provenance: Chalandon Family, Paris
Exhibitions: *Bacchiacca and His Friends,* Baltimore Museum of Art, 1916, No. 85, illustrated on page 56; *Problem Pictures: Paintings without Authors,* Vassar College Art Gallery, Poughkeepsie, 1965, No. 5; *Seven Centuries of Italian Art,* Rhode Island School of Design, 1967.
Several suggestions have been made for the author of this painting: Pier Francesco Foschi, Jacopo da Pontormo, but a firm attribution is still missing. The figure of St. Joseph reminds us of some compositions by Andrea del Sarto but the color and the treatment of drapery make this panel closer to Pontormo.

DOMENICO BECCAFUMI
(Siena ca. 1486-1551)

P2. *The Baptism of Christ*
P3. *A Vision of St. Catherina of Siena*

Oil on panel, both panels, 9 1/2 x 15 inches
Lent by the Philbrook Art Center
Samuel H. Kress Collection
Provenance: Manzi Collection, Siena; Samuel H. Kress Collection, 1939.
Bibliography: *Paintings and Sculpture of the Samuel H. Kress Collection, Philbrook Art Center,* Tulsa, 1953 pp. 38-41, illustrated.
Probably part of a predella, these two panels are accepted as mature works by Beccafumi by G. Fiocco, R. Longhi, F.F.M. Perkins, W. Suida and A. Venturi. There is another painting of *The Baptism of Christ* in the Siena Pinacoteca (No. 344) containing the same elements but of a different, vertical size, where the God the Father is emerging from the clouds. In *A Vision of St. Catherina of Siena,* the saint is offered two crowns: one of roses, the other of thorns; she chooses the thorned one believing that the suffering makes us like unto Him. The delicacy of the colors and the masterly brushwork date these panels to Beccafumi's mature period.

GIOVANNI FRANCESCO BEZZI
called NOSADELLA
(Born in Bologna, died 1571)

P4. *The Holy Family with St. John*

Oil on panel, 19 1/2 x 15 inches
Lent by The Art Association of Indianapolis, The Herron Museum
Provenance: Achillito Chieso, Milan; William Randolf Hearst
This panel was auctioned at the American Art Galleries, New York City on April 16, 1926.
Bibliography: S. E. Ostrow, "Curator's Report," *Art Association of Indianapolis, Bulletin Herron Museum of Art,* V. 53, No. 3, 1966, pp. 56-69,

Fig. 1; *Gazette Des Beaux-Arts,* No. 1176, Fevrier 1967, illustrated.
Bezzi was a pupil of Pellegrino Tibaldi (1527-1595) but we know very little about his life. Bezzi probably worked with his teacher in Bologna and followed him to Milan. While Tibaldi's influence is evident, Bezzi succeeded in creating his own style.

JACOPO CARRUCCI, called IL PONTORMO
(Pontormo 1494-Florence 1557)

P5. *Madonna and Child with Two Angels*

Oil on panel, 40 1/4 x 31 inches
Lent by the M. H. De Young Memorial Museum
Samuel H. Kress Collection
Exhibitions: *Mostra del Pontormo e del primo Manierismo Fiorentino,* Florence, 1956, No. 52, p. 32 illustrated; *Bacchiacca and His Friends,* Baltimore Museum of Art, 1961, No. 54, p. 57, illustrated p. 15.
Bibliography: W. E. Suida, *The Samuel H. Kress Collection,* M. H. De Young Memorial Museum, San Francisco, 1955, p. 52, illustrated.
Pontormo was a pupil of Andrea del Sarto and was influenced by Michelangelo and by Duerer, whose engravings were widely known in Italy at this time. He was one of the creators of the so-called *Primo Manierismo Fiorentino* whose impact on the entire development of Mannerism could hardly be overestimated.
There are two similar versions of this composition: one in the Galleria Corsini, Florence and the other in the collection of Marchese Roberto Pucci, also in Florence. The Corsini picture does not have the child on the left side, while the Pucci panel, being of a lesser quality, has also three children. The Kress painting is dated by W. E. Suida and R. Longhi c. 1523, the time when Pontormo was working on the frescoes in the Certosa di Val d'Ema (1522-25) and there is definitely a stylistic relationship between these two works.

JACOPO CARRUCCI called IL PONTORMO
(Pontormo 1494-Florence 1557)

P6. *Madonna and Child*

Oil on panel, 49 1/2 x 40 1/2 inches
Lent by the Acquavella Galleries, Inc.
Provenance: Ottaviano de Medici Ferrari, Florence; Frascione Collection, Florence Exhibition: *Fontainebleau e la Maniera Italiana,* Naples, 1952, No. 11, illustrated.
There are several known versions of this composition for which, perhaps, we find a reference in Giorgio Vasari's *Vite,* Vasari-Milanesi, 1881, VI, p. 280. This panel is considered by Prof. Roberto Longhi as an "original which does not leave any doubt as to the artist who executed it; it is certainly by Pontormo, and one of his most personal and fascinating creations." Professor Longhi dates this panel about 1520-25, but a date closer to 1530, seems to be more correct. For more details see: F. Goldschmidt, *Pontormo, Rosso*

und Bronzino, Leipzig, 1911 p. 47; **M. F. Clapp,** *Jacopo Carrucci da Pontormo,* New Haven, 1916. Shown only in Binghamton.

AGNOLO BRONZINO, Circle of
16th Century

P7. *Portrait of a Young Lady*

Oil on panel, 27 1/2 x 21 3/8 inches
Inscribed and dated: C. A. C. M.D.LXV. (1565)
Lent by the Seattle Art Museum
Samuel H. Kress Collection
Provenance: Samuel H. Kress Collection, 1947.
Exhibition: *Bacchiacca and His Friends,* Baltimore Museum of Art, 1961, No. 48
Bibliography: *Italian Art, Samuel H. Kress Collection,* Seattle Art Museum, 1952, No. 18, illustrated; *European Paintings and Sculpture, The Samuel H. Kress Collection,* Seattle Art Museum, 1954, p. 48, illustrated.
This excellent portrait, painted with exceptional freedom, has been suggested by W. Suida, C. H. Smyth and M. Modestini as a work by Santi di Tito. The general character of the composition is that of Bronzino, but the pictorial treatment and the way in which Bronzino depicted his portraits are different.

GIROLAMO MACCHIETTI
(Florence c. 1535-1592)

P8. *Holy Family*

Oil on panel, 39 x 30 3/4 inches
Lent by Mr. and Mrs. Robert L. Manning
This panel was attributed by Federico Zeri to Macchietti, who began to paint in the studio of Michele di Ridolfo Ghirlandaio and collaborated later with Vasari on the project for the wedding of Francesco de' Medici and Maria d'Austria in 1565. In the early 1570's Macchietti was working in the *Studiolo of Francesco I* in the Palazzo Vecchio.
The composition of this interesting painting, particularly the figure of St. Joseph, is characteristic of the artists working around Giorgio Vasari. This specific painting is related to the *Adoration of the Magi* by Macchietti in the church of San Lorenzo in Florence.
Shown only in Binghamton.
Unpublished.

FRANCESCO MAZZOLA, called
PARMIGIANINO
(Parma 1503- Casal Maggiore 1540)

P9. *Lorenzo Cybo and His Page*

Oil on canvas, 50 x 41 inches
Inscribed lower right: LAVRENTIVS CYBO MAIC MASSAE ATQVE COMES FERENTILLI ANNO M.D. XXIII (1532)
Lent by the Columbia Museum of Art
Provenance: Contessa Prenfanelli Cybo; Marchese Strozzi (son of Contessa Frenelli Cybo), Florence; Wildenstein & Co., Inc., New York City

Exhibitions: *Italian Paintings,* Wildenstein & Co., New York City, 1947, No. 41; *The Italian Renaissance,* Vancouver Art Gallery, 1953, p. 30; *Pontormo to Greco,* John Herron Art Museum, Indianapolis, 1954, No. 24, illustrated; George T. Hunter Gallery, Chattanooga, Tennessee, 1960.
Bibliography: S. J. Freedberg, *Parmigianino,* Harvard University Press, 1950, pp. 203-204.
Parmigianino was one of the most influential Mannerist painters, whose complex restless diagonal patterns and the erotic character of his gracefully elongated figures, became the typical features of the style.
Lorenzo Cybo was Captain of the Papal Guard and this portrait was painted in Rome. There is another version of this canvas in the Royal Museum of Art, Copenhagen (no. 533), which Freedberg considers an authentic work by Parmigianino and the Columbia picture a copy of it; Berenson and Offner attribute this painting to Parmigianino. Vasari mentioned Captain Cybo as "a very handsome man, who heard the art of Francesco praised and had his portrait painted by him" (Vasari, *Vite,* V. p. 224).

FRANCESCO MAZZOLA
called PARMIGIANINO
(Parma 1503-Casal Maggiore 1540)

P10. *Portrait of a Lady*

Oil on canvas, 43 1/2 x 36 5/8 inches
Lent by Mr. Walter P. Chrysler, Jr.
Provenance: Ercole Coccapani, Modena: Private Collection, New York City; Newhouse Galleries, New York City.
Exhibitions: *Italian Renaissance and Baroque Paintings from the Collection of Walter P. Chrysler, Jr.,* Norfolk Museum of Arts and Sciences, Norfolk, Virginia, 1968, no. 9, p. 13, illustrated.
Bibliography: Count Campori, *Raccolta di cataloghi e inventari inediti,* 1870, p. 149; Lili Froelich-Bum, "An Unknown Portrait by Parmigianino," *Pantheon,* XVIII, May 1960, pp. 114-115, illustrated.
According to Froelich-Bum this portrait must represent a great lady as it is proven by her ellegant attire and her hairdress and dates this magnificent portrait about 1535.

FRANCESCO MORANDINI, called
IL POPPI
(Poppi 1544-Florence 1597)

P11. *The Deposition*

Oil on panel, 47 7/8 x 34 1/2 inches
Lent by Mr. Edmund Pillsbury
Il Poppi was a friend of Giorgio Vasari with whom he worked in 1565 on the project for the wedding of Francesco de Medici and Giovanna of Austria. He also participated in the decoration of the *Studiolo of Francesco I* in the Palazzo Vecchio between 1570-73. In his early work Il Poppi shows an influence of Parmigianino (particularly in the *Studiolo* decoration representing *Alexander the Great*

Giving Campaspe to Apelles) but later turned more toward the style of Pontormo and Vasari.
Unpublished.

LELIO ORSI
(Reggio c. 1511-Novellara 1587)

P12. *Noli Me Tangere*

Oil on canvas, 36 x 29 1/2 inches
Lent by the Wadsworth Atheneum
Sumner Fund, 1936
Provenance: Chiesa Collection, Milan, Italy; Ehrich Galleries, New York City; Durlacher Brothers, New York City
Exhibitions: Hartford, Conn., Wadsworth Atheneum, *Night Scenes*, 1940, No. 13 in cat.; Hartford, Conn., Wadsworth Atheneum, *Life of Christ*, 1948, No. 155 in cat.; Indianapolis, Ind., The John Herron Art Institute, *Pontormo to Greco*, 1954, No. 32, illustrated; *In Handbook*, 1958, pg. 30; repr.; Sarasota, Florida, John and Mable Ringling Museum of Art, *A. Everett Austin, Jr.: A Director's Taste and Achievement*, 1958, No. 59 in cat.; *ibid*, Hartford, Conn., Wadsworth Atheneum, 1958
Bibliography: T. Kunze, "Lelio Orsi" in Thieme-Becker, *Kuenstler-Lexikon*, Leipzig, 1932, XXVI, pp. 58-59; R. Salvini, *Mostra di Lelio Orsi*, Reggio Emilia, 1950, p. 163 as formerly Chiesa Collection, now in America.

We know very little about the life and work of Orsi, and, as a matter of fact, there is not a painting recorded or signed by him. From the attributed works are evident his debts to Michelangelo, Correggio and Northern artists.
Noli Me Tangere is a typical painting by Orsi in which the exaggeration of the proportions, elongated figures and fantastic landscape, also characterize the Mannerist style. R. Longhi records a drawing for this painting in the Fourche Collection in the Orleans Museum (see above mentioned article by I. Kunze, p. 59).

SCIPIONE PULZONE, called
IL GAETANO
(Gaeta c. 1550-Rome 1598)

P.13 *Portrait of a Lady*

Oil on canvas, 18 3/4 x 14 1/2 inches
Lent by Mr. Victor D. Spark
Provenance: Mary E. Tirudy
Exhibitions: *Pontormo to Greco,* John Herron Art Museum, Indianapolis, 1954, No. 20, illustrated (as Alessandro Allori); The Joe and Emily Lowe Art Gallery, University of Miami, Coral Gables, 1956; Columbia Museum of Art, Columbia, 1956.
Bibliography: F. Zeri, *Pittura e controriforma*, Torino, 1957, reproduced on cover and illustrated No. 86.
Most of his mature period Pulzone spent in Rome but several visits to Florence made him aware of the happenings in this city. He was best known for his portraits but also executed some religious paintings in which he emphasized the Mannerist extravagance in color and design typical of the period.
Friedlaender attributed this painting to Allori and

as such was exhibited in Indianapolis; the attribution to Pulzone by F. Zeri is correct and this painting has all the characteristics of the Pulzone fashionable portraits.
A very similar portrait of the same personality and evidently by the same hand was sold in London (Christie's, *Fine Paintings by Old Masters,* July 26, 1968, no. 92, illustrated), as Florentine, circa 1580 and the sitter was identified as "Anne of Austria," the daughter of Phillip III of Spain. Anne of Austria died in 1566, and therefore this could not be a portrait representing her. I am grateful to Robert L. Manning for bringing this information to my attention.

FRANCESCO DEI ROSSI, called
FRANCESCO SALVIATI
(Florence 1510-Rome 1563)

P14. *Portrait of a Gentleman*

Oil on canvas, 48 1/2 x 36 3/4 inches
Lent by the Metropolitan Museum of Art
Gift of Mr. and Mrs. Nate B. Spingold, 1955
Provenance: John E. Taylor, London (until 1905); Mrs. John E. Taylor, London, 1912; Colnaghi and Co., London, 1912; M. Knoedler and Co., New York, 1913; J. Horace Harding, New York, 1913-40; James St. L. O'Toole Gallery, New York, 1940.
Exhibitions: *Twenty Masterpieces (1400-1800),* M. Knoedler and Co., 1935, No. 25; *Pontormo to Greco,* John Herron Art Museum, Indianapolis, 1954. No. 18. illustrated.
Bibliography: Christie's Sale, London, July 5-8, 1912, No. 28; "A Salviati in a Portrait Exhibition," *Connoisseur,* vol. 105, 1940, p. 76.
Salviati studied with Andrea del Sarto and during his activity in Florence became a close friend of Vasari, who in a detailed biographical note in his *Vite* describes the neurotic behaviour of Salviati. Most of his mature activity Salviati divided between Florence and Rome and some shorter visits to Venice and France and he worked with a variety of media and subjects: oil, fresco, designer of tapestries, altarpieces and portraits. His adopted name he took from the Cardinal Salviati, who was one of his first patrons.
In this portrait Salviati, who with such brilliancy depicts an almost mirror-image of his sitter, shows his great ability as a portrait painter.

JAN VAN DER STRAET, called
STRADANUS
(Bruges 1523-Florence 1605)

P15. *The Charity of St. Nicholas*

Oil on panel, 25 3/8 x 38 1/8 inches
Lent by the Columbia Museum of Art
Samuel H. Kress Collection
Provenance: Countess Reppi, Rome(?); Count Contini-Bonacossi, Rome; Samuel H. Kress Collection, 1930
Exhibitions: *Exhibition of Italian Paintings,* shown in 24 American cities, 1932-35, p. 22, illustrated; National Gallery of Art, Washington, 1941-52; *Art Treasures for America,* National Gallery of Art, Washington, 1961-62, no. 23.

Bibliography: F. Antal, *Zur Problems des nieder-laendischen Manierisms* in *Kritische Berichte zur Kunstgeschichtlichen Literatur,* Berlin, 1928-29, Heft 3/4, p. 226 (as Pitro Candido); *Preliminary Catalogue,* National Gallery of Art, Washington, 1941, p. 100 (as Florentine School); W. Suida, *Art of the Italian Renaissance from the Samuel H. Kress Collection,* Columbia Museum of Art, 1954, p. 41, No. 16; G. Emerson, *The Kress Collection, The National Geographic Magazine,* Vol. 120, No. 6, Dec. 1961, p. 840; A. Contini-Bonacossi, *Renaissance Art from the Samuel H. Kress Collection,* Columbia Museum of Art, Columbia, 1962, pp. 44-47, No. 15, illustrated (as Pietro Candido); *Handzeichnungen alter Meister aus schweizer Privatbesitz,* Kunsthalle Bremen, 1967, p. 46, No. 62; L. Berti, *Il Principe dello studiolo,* Florence, 1967, ill. 173.

Stradanus began to work with Maximilian Franck in 1535 and studied also with Pieter Aersten between 1537 and 1540. Probably in 1545 Stradanus went to Italy first with a short stop in Venice then to Florence, where he met Vasari. He was employed on several projects in Florence including the extensive works in the Palazzo Vecchio. Stradanus' style affected several artists working in Florence, including Giorgio Vasari, and his Flemish taste for the *grotesque,* particularly evident in the *Christ Driving the Merchants from the Temple,* now in the church of Santo Spirito in Florence, never left him completely.

This painting represents an episode in the life of the Saint as told by Jacobus a Varagine in his *Golden Legend.* We see the Saint about to throw the golden balls to the daughters of an impoverished nobleman, who was not able to provide the dowry for his daughters. This legend still survives in some European countries, where on the eve of the Saint Nicholas' day, December 6, the children are given the gifts.

The drawing for this painting (no. P15a) is in the collection of Kurt Meissner, Zurich (see: F. Forster-Hahn, *Old Master Drawings from the collection of Kurt Meissner.* exhibition catalogue, Stanford Art Book 10, 1969, No. 29, 11 3/16 x 16 7/8 inches, brush and bistre heightened in the white; I am grateful to Mr. Robert L. Manning for bringing to my attention this catalogue and for providing the photograph of it). This drawing, as well as the painting, were originally attributed to different artists: Niccolo dell'Abbate, Empoli, Florentine School, ca. 1540, and Pietro Candido. The attribution of Prof. Ferdinando Bologna and L. Berti to Stradanus seems to be the right one. There is also a 16th century engraving (J. D. Passavant, *Le Peintre-Engraveur,* Leipzig, 1860-64, Vol. VI, p. 156, No. 21), of which two prints exist in the Samuel H. Kress Foundation (no. P15b) and the Metropolitan Museum of Art.

SANTI DI TITO
(Borgo San Sepolcro 1536-Florence 1603)

P16. *Portrait of a Young Man*

Oil on panel, 44 x 33 inches
Lent by Mr. Walter P. Chrysler, Jr.

Provenance: Medici Collection, Florence; Riccardi Collection, Florence; Wengraf, Old Masters Gallery, London
Exhibitions: Bertina Suida Manning, *1550-1650 A Century of Masters from the Collection of Walter P. Chrysler, Jr.,* Ft. Worth Art Center, Ft. Worth, Texas; Philbrook Art Center, Tulsa, Oklahoma; University of Texas, Austin, 1962-63, p. 46, illustrated p. 32; Robert L. Manning, *Italian Renaissance and Baroque Paintings from the Collection of Walter P. Chrysler, Jr.,* Norfolk Museum of Arts and Sciences, Norfolk, Virginia, 1968, p. 22, No. 17, illustrated.

Santi di Tito first studied with Sebastiano da Montecarlo and also with Baccio Bandinelli and Angelo Bronzino. He was one of the important younger Mannerists, who in spite of the evident influence by Bronzino, succeeded in developing his own style. In 1558 Santi di Tito went to Rome and worked on several projects. In 1564 he returned to Florence and was commissioned to work on Michelangelo's funeral. His later style became more academic as compared with the rest of the artists working around Vasari.

Bertina Suida Manning correctly recognized an influence by Bronzino but suggested a strong individual approach by Santi: "more direct and with fewer psychological complications." Also this portrait has some resemblance with known portraits of Francesco de Medici, particularly with a portrait by Bronzino, which appeared on the New York market in 1957, in "the shape of the head, the line of the eyebrows, the nose, the mouth, even the ears."

GIORGIO VASARI
(Arezzo 1511-Florence 1574)

P17. *Annunciation*

Oil on panel, 26 3/4 x 33 inches
Lent by the University of Notre Dame Art Gallery
Provenance: Collection of Charles A. Wightman
Bibliography: *Catalogue of the Wightman Memorial Art Gallery," Bulletin of the University of Notre Dame,* Vol. XXIX, No. 4, 1934, p. 107; E. Pillsbury, "Three Unpublished Paintings by Giorgio Vasari," *The Burlington Magazine,* February 1970, pp. 94-101, illustrated.

Since on many occasions in this catalogue reference will be made to the works and life of Giorgio Vasari, we will in this first entry record only the most essential information.

Giorgio Vasari began his artistic career in the studio of Guglielmo di Pietro de Marcillat, a glass and fresco painter in Arezzo. In 1524 Vasari left for Florence through the help of Cardinal Silvio Passerinini and met Salviati, Andrea del Sarto and Baccio Bandinelli. In 1527 he returned to Arezzo after the expulsion of the Medicis from Florence, but in 1529 Vasari was again in Florence. Following an invitation by Cardinal Ippolito de' Medici in 1531, Vasari left for Rome where he studied extensively the works of Michelangelo, Raphael, and Peruzzi. In 1532 he returned to Florence working for Alessandro and Ottaviano Medici, where he began his prolific career as a painter and architect.

After some works in Rome, near Bologna and Venice, Vasari began the decoration of his house in Arezzo, Casa Vasari, in 1542. Two years later Vasari finished the decoration of a sala in the Cancelleria in Rome with the scenes from the life of the Pope Paul III; in the same year he started to work on his *Vite*. Vasari married **Niccolosa** Bacci in 1549 and finally moved with his family to Florence in 1554-55, where he started to work in the service of Cosimo I de' Medici on the Palazzo Vecchio. Until his death Vasari was directly or indirectly involved in all of the important decorative or building projects in Florence and Rome. A friend of Michelangelo and of the most illustrious Florentines, Vasari become a central artistic figure and a leading connoisseur of the arts, as evidenced in his *Vite,* a monumental work on artists and arts from Cimabue to Titian.

The *Annunciation* panel entered the collection of the University of Notre Dame in 1924 as a gift of Charles A. Wightman and was called *Florentine School.* Prof. Zeri attributed the panel to Vasari and this attribution was also accepted by Edmund Pillsbury as an early work. Probably painted in the early 1540s, this painting could be compared with an engraving by Marco Dente da Ravenna (no. G2) traditionally attributed to be a copy after a lost work by Raphael. Pillsbury also has rightly pointed to the precedents of this composition in the works of Salviati (*Annunciation* in the S. Francesco a Ripa, Rome) and Perino del Vaga (*Annunciation* in the Pucci Chapel in S. Trinita dei Monti).

While in this early *Annunciation* Vasari puts the emphasis on the interior with all the accessories, rather than on the figures, a manner familiar in the Flemish paintings (see Stradanus, no. P15), in the Louvre *Annunciation* (No. 732) a later work, done for the high altar in the church of S. Maria Novella in Arezzo, the figures play a dominant role.

GIORGIO VASARI
(Arezzo 1511-Florence 1574)

P18. *The Temptation of St. Jerome*

Oil on panel, 65 3/8 x 47 1/2 inches
Lent by The Art Institute of Chicago
Collection: Charles H. and Mary F. S. Worcester
Vasari recorded in his *Vite* (ed. Milanesi, Vol. VII, p. 669) that he "did a Venus and a Leda for M. Ottaviano de' Medici from the cartoons of Michelangelo and a life-size St. Jerome in penitence, contemplating a crucifix and beating his breast, to drive away the lascivious thoughts that beset him in the wilderness, as he himself relates. To indicate this I did Venus fleeing with Cupid in her arms and leading Play, the quiver and arrows strewing the ground." Two other versions of this subject are known : one in the Pitti Palace and the other in the Leeds City Art Gallery in England. The Pitti and Leeds versions are very similar to each other, the Chicago version shows several deviations from the other two (see no. P18a) and this is perhaps the reason that the

Chicago version was questioned in the past as an authentic Vasari. The smaller figures in the Chicago version and a more sketchy approach might be that Vasari changed the first idea and decided to introduce the figures on a more monumental scale and eliminate the elaborate landscape, replace the doves and add the Cupid in the upper right corner.
Shown only in Notre Dame.
Unpublished

GIORGIO VASARI
(Arezzo 1511-Florence 1574)

P19. *St. Mary Magdalen*

Oil on panel, 34 3/8 x 25 5/8 inches
Lent by the Museum of Fine Arts of Houston
Collection: Samuel H. Kress
Provenance: Collection of Duke of Lorraine
Bibliography: W. E. Suida, *The Samuel H. Kress Collection at the Museum of Fine Arts of Houston,* 1953, p. 29, pl. 11
Dr. Suida dated this painting around 1560 and considers it a *typical of the fully developed Florentine mannerist style in the mobility of the figure as well as in the changeable, shimmering colors.*
Shown only in Notre Dame.

GIORGIO VASARI
(Arezzo 1511-Florence 1574)

P.20 *Holy Family*

Oil on panel, 51 1/4 x 34 1/ inches
Lent by an Anonymous Collector
Provenance: Galleria Corsini, Florence
Bibliography: *Galleria Corsini,* catalogue, Vol. VII, p. 262 (n.d.); *Galleria Principi Corsini,* Firenze, 1886, p. 29, no. 96.
The additions to all four sides of this painting have been removed and the *Holy Family* is reproduced here in its original size; the Brogi photograph No. 17642 clearly indicates the removed parts.
As in the *Holy Family* by an Anonymous painter (no. P1) in this painting we note the influence of Vasari's teacher, Andrea del Sarto, particularly reflected in the figure of St. Joseph.
Shown only in Binghamton.

GIORGIO VASARI
(Arezzo 1511-Florence 1574)

P21. *Abraham and Melchizedek*

Oil on canvas, 23 5/8 x 17 1/8 inches
Lent by the Bob Jones University Collection
Provenance: Havemeyer Collection, New York City; Weitzner Collection
Exhibitions: *Bacchiacca and His Friends,* Baltimore Museum of Art, 1961, p. 64, No. 74
Bibliography: *Art Quarterly,* Spring 1961, p. 94, illustrated; *Bob Jones University Catalogue of the Art Collection,* Volume I, Italian and French Paintings, 1962, pp. 91-92, illustrated
This painting is attributed to Vasari by Dr. Suida and Prof. Zeri and could be related in style and composition to the *Conversion of Saul* in the San Pitro in Montorio dated in the early 1550s.

M.M.

P2. *The Baptism of Christ*   DOMENICO BECCAFUMI

P3. *A Vision of St. Catherina of Siena*   DOMENICO BECCAFUMI

P4. *The Holy Family with St. John*

GIOVANNI FRANCESCO BEZZI,
called NOSADELLA

P5. *Madonna and Child with Two Angels*   JACOPO CARRUCCI,
                                                            called IL PONTORMO

·C · A · C · M · D · LXV·

P7. *Portrait of a Young Lady*   AGNOLO BRONZINO, Circle of

P8. *Holy Family*   GIROLAMO MACCHIETTI

P9. *Lorenzo Cybo and His Page*

FRANCESCO MAZZOLA
called PARMIGIANINO

P11. *The Deposition*

FRANCESCO MORANDINI
called IL POPPI

P12. *Noli Me Tangere*   LELIO ORSI

P13. *Portrait of a Lady*   SCIPIONE PULZONE

P14. *Portrait of a Gentleman*   FRANCESCO SALVIATI

P15.   *The Charity of Saint Nicholas*   STRADANUS

P15a. *The Charity of Saint Nicholas*   **STRADANUS**
       Courtesy of Mr. Kurt Meissner, Zurich

P15b. *The Charity of Saint Nicholas*   **STRADANUS**
       Engraving, 10 3/4 x 15 3/4 inches
       Courtesy of the Samuel H. Kress Foundation

P16. *Portrait of a Young Man*   SANTI DI TITO

P18a. *The Temptation of St. Jerome*
Palazzo Pitti

GIORGIO VASARI
(Photo: Alinari)

P19. *St. Mary Magdalen*   GIORGIO VASARI

P20. *Holy Family*   GIORGIO VASARI

P21. *Abraham and Melchizedek*   GIORGIO VASARI

The Role of the Concept of *Disegno* in Mid-Sixteenth Century Florence

Of all the terms relevant to Italian mid-sixteenth century aesthetics, *disegno* is perhaps the most fundamental.[1] In connection with this exhibition, it is fitting to consider its significance to Florentine artists and theorists of the period. Roughly, although inadequately, translatable as "design," the word has acquired a complexity of meaning at least as challenging as that of its English counterpart.[2] It is thus appropriate to begin this study with a discussion of the major connotations carried by the term in mid-sixteenth century Italy. These connotations have been touched upon by modern scholarship,[3] but those most significant for the period— namely the association of *disegno* with composition, with proportion, and with beauty—have not so far received adequate attention. The present essay re-examines and reassesses this association.

The Meaning of *Disegno*

Throughout the Renaissance, the most elementary connotations of *disegno* and its verb *disegnare* concerned the activity of drawing, the skill in that activity, and the resultant product. A *disegno*, in this context, was simply "a drawing," a representation made up of outlines and, where present, light and shade.

The situation was different when it came to apply the terms to painting. The tendency here was to view light and shade in intimate relationship with color, and to consider the *disegno* as residing solely in the outlines. We find this view already fully developed in the Quattrocento. When establishing the subdivisions of painting, Alberti for example, through the expression *circumscriptione*, strictly identified *disegno* with outlining: "circumscription is nothing but the *disegniamento* of the border . . . a good circumscription, that is, a good *disegno*. . . . Having then finished circumscription, that is, the mode of *disegnare* . . ." [la circumscriptione è non altro che disegniamento del orlo . . .[4] uno buona circumscriptione, cioè uno buono disegnio[5] . . . Finita adunque la circumscrittione, cioè il modo del disegniare[6] . . .] Similarly, Piero della Francesca stated that "By *disegno* we mean the profiles and contours which are contained in the thing." [Desegno intendiamo essere profili et contorni che nella cosa se contene][7].

Since the Albertian notion of *disegno* in relation to painting is of significance for an understanding of the concept of *disegno* in mid-sixteenth century, we shall investigate it more carefully. In so doing, we shall consider the outline with respect to two of its basic functions.

One of these functions is to set or establish a boundary to a form. Far from recommending a rigid, two-dimensional border, Alberti insisted that this boundary be smoothed out almost to extinction. For him, indeed, a good *disegno* meant first of all an outline which suggested continuity of the surface around the three-dimensional form represented: "Circumscription will describe the turning of the border in the painting . . . I thus say that this circumscription ought to be made up of lines most subtle, almost such as will tend to escape notice . . . Because circumscription is nothing but the *disegniamento* of the border, which, when done with too apparent a line, will not indicate a margin of surface but a break, and I would wish that, in circumscribing, only the movement of the border be captured. In which thing, I affirm one ought to exercise a great deal. No composition and no reception of lights can be praised, where there not be a good circumscription added. And not seldom does one see a good circumscription, that is, a good *disegno*, by itself to be most pleasant." [Sarà circumscriptione quella che descriva l'attorniare dell' orlo nella pictura. . . . Io così dico in questa circonscriptione molto doversi observare ch'ella sia di linee sottilissime fatta, quasi tali che fuggano essere vedute. . . . Però che la circonscriptione è non altro che disegniamento del orlo quale, ove sia fatto con linea troppo apparente, non dimostrerà ivi essere margine di superficie ma fessura et io desidererei nulla proseguirsi circonscrivendo che solo l'andare del orlo. In qual cosa così affermo debbano molto exercitarsi. Niuna compositione et niuno ricevere di lumi si può lodare ove non sia buona circonscriptione aggiunta. Et non raro pur si vede solo una buona circonscriptione, cioè uno buono disegnio, per se essere gratissimo].[8]

A second basic function of the outline is to compose a form. By this is meant that the outline, in going around the form on the two-dimensional surface, builds it up, as it were, and structures it. In so doing, the outline accomplishes several things: in the case of the human figure for instance, it articulates the limbs and establishes the posture of the figure; it also establishes its proportions.

In the eyes of Alberti and indeed of virtually all Renaissance theorists, the establishment of proportions was of central importance, for they considered harmony of proportions the chief component of artistic beauty.[9] Let us simply note here that for Alberti this task, which in some respects constituted the core of the compositional function of the outline, did not strictly belong to *circumscriptione* or *disegno*. It pertained to a broader activity dealing with the composition of the painting as a whole, and which he had appropriately entitled *compositione*. Thus we read, under this heading: "First one ought to make sure that all the members agree well. They will agree when in size, function, kind, color and other similar things they correspond to a unified beauty." [Conviensi inprima dare opera che tutti i membri bene convengano. Converrano quando et di grandezza et d'offitio et di spetie et di colore et d'altre simili cose corresponderanno ad una bellezza].[10]

The sixteenth century substantially modified the Albertian approach to painting. It recognized the compositional function of the outline, especially the establishment of proportions, as fully pertaining to *disegno*. When convenient, it also admitted under *disegno* the compositional aspects of light and shade, so that the total anatomical constitution of the human figure could be evaluated in terms of *disegno*. As a corollary to the first of these theoretical transformations, the concept of harmonious proportion, central to the notion of artistic beauty, found itself brought under the direct jurisdiction of *disegno*.

The first attempt to codify this Cinquecento view was made by the Venetian Paolo Pino in 1548 in his *Dialogo di Pittura*. Rejecting Alberti's division, Pino substituted the henceforth standard one of *disegno*, invention (*invenzione*), and coloring (*colorire*).[11] He then proceeded to subdivide *disegno* into judgment (*giudicio*), circumscription (*circumscrizzione*), practice (*pratica*), and composition (*composizione*). Of *composizione*, and thus of *disegno*, he wrote: "In it are included all the others, that is, judgment, circumscription, and practice, since this correct composition consists in the complete forming of the surfaces, which are part of the members, and of the members as part of the body, and of the body, then, as wholeness of the work." [In questa s'include tutte l'altre, cioè il giudicio, la circoscrizzione e la pratica, imperò che questa retta composizione consiste nel formar integramente le superfizie, le quali sono parti de' membri, et i membri come parte del corpo, il corpo, poi, come integrità dell'opera].[12] He then added, still referring to *composizione* and therefore to *disegno:* "It gives the right portion to the whole." [Questa dà la giusta porzione al tutto.][13] Earlier in the *Dialogo*, Pino had identified "right portion" (*giusta porzione*) with harmonious proportion and had even given a set of measurements with which to achieve it.[14]

Interestingly enough, a second attempt to penetrate into the more fundamental function of *disegno* was soon made by another Venetian, Ludovico Dolce. In his *Dialogo della Pittura* of 1557, Dolce, like Pino, subdivides painting into *disegno*, invention and coloring.[15] More openly than his predecessor, Dolce discusses proportion under *disegno*, like him giving a set of measurements for the ideal human body. [16] He eventually comes to the conclusion that "proportion, then, being the main foundation of *disegno*, he who will observe the former better will be, in the latter, a better master." [essendo adunque il principal fondamento del disegno la proporzione, chi questa meglio osserverà fia in esso miglior maestro].[17] This was tantamount to asserting that a master in *disegno* was first and foremost a master of proportions.

Neither Pino's reworking of Alberti's division nor Dolce's remarks were dictated by mere literary fantasy. The concepts of composition, proportion, and beauty lie indeed at the core of the broader notion of *disegno* in mid-sixteenth century. It is, for instance, essentially around these concepts that Vasari's definition and discussion of *disegno* in the preface to the third part of the *Lives* revolve: *"Disegno* was the imitation of the most beautiful of nature in all the figures . . ." [Il disegno fu lo imitare il più bello della natura in tutte le figure . . .].[18] As applied to the painter, the contemporary expression *aver disegno* (which meant to be skilled in *disegno*) would then refer to his talent primarily in the composition of the individual human figure (chiefly through the outline, to be sure).[19] In reference to the finished painting, on the other hand, the expression would correspondingly allude to its compositional excellence (chiefly linear), especially as realized in the forms individually considered. Dolce certainly had this quality in mind when he equated *disegno* and beauty in the following way: "about whatever thing, wishing to signify that it is beautiful, one says that it has *disegno*." [di qualunque cosa, volendo significar che ella sia bella, si dice lei aver disegno].[20] The textual identification of *disegno* with harmonious proportion eventually came with the Milanese theoretician G. P. Lomazzo, whose *Idea del Tempio* of 1590 stated that: "The foundation of the whole . . . upon which every thing rests as on a base of the greatest firmness, and from which derives all the beauty, is that which the Greeks call Eurythmy and we name *disegno*." [Il fondamento di tutto . . . sopra il quale ogni cosa come sopra saldissima base si riposa, ed onde deriva tutta la bellezza, è quello che i Greci chiamano Euritmia e noi nominiamo disegno].[21]

The viewing of the *disegno* of a painting in compositional terms had an important effect on the theoretical attitude towards the three-dimensional arts. It stimulated a new awareness of the linearity embodied in the media of sculpture and architecture, and chiefly through this awareness it allowed a free extension of the term *disegno* and of its more pregnant connotations to these media.

Disegno had indeed been occasionally used by Quattrocento writers in reference to three-dimensional forms, but rather timidly. As regards architecture, for instance, *disegno* and *disegnare* had tended to refer exclusively to the preparatory drawing and to its layout in the drawing medium.[22] Alberti had, however, described how one could look at a building as a three-dimensional construction of lines (or, one might say, as a three-dimensional linear construction) independently of the matter, and recognize the same construction in buildings identically structured. Writing in Latin, he had given this construction the name *lineamentum,* and this was plainly translated as *disegno* in the 1550 Italian edition: "Neither has the *disegno* in itself the disposition to follow matter, but it is such that we know that the same *disegno* is in an infinite number of buildings, if only we see in them a same form, that is, if only their parts, and the site, and their orders be in everything similar among themselves in lines and angles." [Ne hà il disegno in se instinto di seguitare la Materia, ma è tale che noi conosciamo che il medesimo disegno è in infiniti edificii, pur' che noi veggiamo in essi una medesima forma, cioè pur' che le parti loro, & il sito, & gli ordini di quelle siano in tutto simili infra loro di linee, & di angoli][23]

If then the finished building could be seen as embodying a *disegno,* and now that *disegno* had decisively come to be viewed in compositional terms, the path was entirely open to a qualitative discussion of the building itself in terms of *disegno.* Thus we see Vasari remark about the leaning Tower of Pisa, no doubt referring, in the expression *disegno,* to its compositional qualities and specifically to its proportions: "it is praised, not because it has *disegno* or beautiful manner, but only because of its extravagance, not seeming to the viewer that it could in any way sustain itself." [è lodato, non perchè abbia in sè disegno o bella maniera, ma solamente per la sua stravaganza, non parendo a chi lo vede che egli possa in niuna guisa sostenersi].[24] In the same mode of interpretation, an architect could be rated in terms of *disegno* according to his greater or lesser sense of composition. Here again Vasari provides the example: "in our times certain plebeian architects, presumptuous and without *disegno,* have made almost carelessly, without observing decorum, art, or any order, all their things monstruous and worse than the German." [hanno a' tempi nostri certi architetti plebei, prosontuosi e senza disegno, fatto quasi a caso, senza servar decoro, arte o ordine nessuno, tutte le cose loro mostruose e peggio che le tedesche].[25]

A related development can be observed as regards sculpture. We do come upon direct connections between *disegno* and sculptured forms, in Quattrocento literature, but they remain rare and generally restricted to relief depictions. A fully isolated sculptured form could, however, be viewed as made up of outlines in a way comparable to a painted one. According to Leonardo da Vinci, the painter's and sculptor's tasks were identical precisely in this outline aspect: "The sculptor seeks only the outlines that surround the carved matter, and the painter seeks the same outlines and aside from these he seeks light and shade, color, and foreshortening, in which things nature constantly helps the sculptor." [Lo scultore solo ricerca i lineamenti, che circondano la materia sculta, et il pittore ricerca li medesimi lineamenti et oltre à quelli ricerca ombra e lume, colore, e scorto, delle quali cose la natura n'aiuta di continuo lo scultore][26] The sixteenth century painter Bronzino similarly considered the art of sculpture as consisting solely in the handling of the outlines: "the art consists only in the lines that surround the body, which [lines] are on the surface" [solo è dell'arte le linee che circondano detto corpo, le quali sono in superficie].[27] Within this conception, a sculptured form in the round could then be viewed as possessing or lacking *disegno* basically in the same way as a painted one. Thus Vasari could write about Michelangelo's *Pietà* in St. Peter's: "to which work let no sculptor, nor rare artist, ever think that he could add in *disegno* or in grace." [alla quale opera non pensi mai scultore, nè artefice raro, potere aggiugnere di disegno nè di grazia].[28] Likewise, a sculptor could be legitimately discussed as possessing or lacking *disegno* without any necessary allusion to his talent as a draftsman, but with specific reference to his ability to properly compose the human figure (individually considered) in his own sphere. It is strictly in agreement with this interpretation that Francesco da Sangallo expressed the following: "any sculptor needs to have, not like the painter, excellent *disegno*, but more, if more be possible, with respect to the diversity of the statues which he makes; because, as I would say, in regards to the nude which the painter will make, the sculptor, wishing to make the same, is required to make many in a single one, with respect to the numerous views, since at every successive glance the round statue becomes another. Thus the painter with a unique view makes a unique figure, and the sculptor in a unique figure makes many with respect to the many views, as I said above. And returning, I say that it will be necessary for the sculptor to have more *disegno*" [qualunque statuario gli bisogna avere, non come allo pittore, bonissimo disegno, ma più, se più possibile fussi, rispetto alla diversità delle statue che lui fa; ché come dissi, lo ignudo che farà lo pittore, volendo lo scultore fare il medesimo, gniene conviene fare molti in un solo, rispetto alle molte viste, ché a ogni volta d'occhio la statua tonda diventa un'altra, in modo che lo pittore (d')una sola vista fa una sola figura, e lo scultore in una sola figura ne fa molte rispetto alle molte viste, come sopra narrai; e tornando, dico che allo scultore gli saria necessario avere più disegno].[29]

The definitive inclusion of the compositional aspect of the outline under the aegis of *disegno*, and the full extension of this concept to the media of sculpture and architecture, contributed to the advent of an important notion: that of an art of *disegno* distinct from, although based upon, the one strictly associated with the drawing medium; a generic art form embracing all three arts of painting, sculpture, and architecture. The fundamental element involved in this *arte del disegno* is still—as in the case of drawing—line. But whereas in drawing we are dealing with lines traced with a drawing instrument, the lines involved in the new *arte del disegno* are those which we observe in the finished product, be the latter a painting, a sculpture, or a building. *Arte del disegno*, in its new sense, may therefore justifiably be called the art of "linear construction," or of "linear structure." Whoever practices the art of architecture, sculpture, or painting could thus be said to practice the art of "linear construction," irrespective of whether he uses preparatory drawings or not—simply because he is concerned with the creation, in whatever medium, of linear constructions (or linear structures). It is with this concept in mind, however confused, that the sculptor Vincenzo Danti could thus define *arte del disegno:* "I say that this art of *disegno* is the one which, as a genus, includes under itself the three most noble arts of architecture, sculpture, and painting of which each one, by itself, is like a species of it." [Quest'arte, dico, del disegno è quella che, come genere, comprende sotto di sé le tre nobilissime arti architettura, scultura e pittura, delle quali ciascuna, per sé stessa, è come specie di quella].[30]

There was room for confusion, especially because all three arts generally made use of drawing; and confusion did indeed generally prevail. The expression *le arti del disegno* (the arts of *disegno*), for instance, could mean either the arts that use the drawing medium or the arts concerned with the creation of linear constructions —or, most generally, an inextricable mixture of the two. Similarly, *disegno* as the foundation of painting, sculpture, and architecture could be interpreted as drawing or as linear structure, irrespective of the medium in which this linear structure is embodied. It is the latter sense that Francesco da Sangallo clearly alluded to when he wrote: "I say that it will be necessary for the sculptor to have more *disegno;* and since the latter is the foundation of every art, not only of these, it follows that sculpture is more difficult in this respect" [dico che allo scultore gli saria necessario avere più disegno, lo quale, per essere il fondamento d'ogni arte, non solo di queste, ne seguita che la scultura in questo è più difficile].[31]

As a result of the transformations that we have been discussing, *disegno* provided a banner under which architects, sculptors, and painters could unite. This solidarity through *disegno* is expressed in the way all three came to be generically referred to as *Artefici del Disegno*[32] (and later as *Professori del Disegno*), and in the way all came to be grouped cohesively in the *Accademia del Disegno*.[33] This Academy, founded in Florence by Vasari in 1563, was the first association of its kind and the ancestor of all the later academies and schools of "design."

It remains true that drawing was the instrument common to all these artists and that the teachings of the Academy seem to have been intended to center on the discipline of drawing (therefore partly justifying the term). But the new connotations acquired by *disegno*—whereby in painting, sculpturing, or in devising a work of architecture one was creating a linear construction (or a linear structure) in which, specifically in its proportions, resided the core of potential beauty—undoubtedly played an important role in bringing about a *disegno* coalition on such a scale. A significant clue to this is given in the Code of Rules of the Accademia, where the organization is referred to as the *Accademia dell'Arte del Disegno* and where, in the opening article, *l'arte del disegno* is unambiguously referred to in generic terms and not as the art of drawing: "Having, the year 1239 (sic), considered the masters, who were then the heads of the art of *disegno*, that its birth and first restoration was due, in architecture, to M. Arnolfo di Lapo, excellent architect, in the building of S.Maria del Fiore, and to M. Giotto di Bondone da Vespignano, who was then the guiding light in drawing (*disegno*), painting, and mosaic, and to M. Andrea di Nino Pisano, most excellent master of sculpture and bronze casting; and as heads of these most noble arts. . . . " [Havendo l'anno 1239 considerato i maestri, i quali furono allhora capi dell'arte del disegno, che la sua nascita et prima rinovatione fu nell'Architectura per M.o Arnolfo di Lapo architetto ecc. te nella fabbrica di Santa Maria del Fiore, e per M.o Giotto di Bondone da Vespignano, allhora prima luce del disegno, della pittura et del mosaico, et per M.o Andrea di Nino Pisano nella scoltura e nel getto del bronzo m.o ecc.mo; e come capi di queste nobilissime arti. . . .].[34]

The New Status of Drawings

Throughout the Trecento and the early part of the Quattrocento, most of the preparatory drawing activity in the creation of a painting took place on its support.[35] Indeed, the number of preliminary drawings on paper was certainly limited, a fact that partially explains the scarcity of such extant drawings. This scarcity may be accounted for by yet another factor: the contemporary lack of interest in the preparatory stages of a painting. Drawing tended to be considered totally subservient to the finished product. As a rule, preparatory studies on paper were not found more worthy of independent preservation than the studies that remained buried beneath the paint. Although some were retained in the workshop for future reference or for the purpose of study, most would have been discarded in the belief that their value had ceased with the completion of the painting.

The introduction of the cartoon, in mid-Quattrocento, altered this situation by establishing drawing on paper as the natural medium for the preparation especially of the fresco. At first limited to single figures, the cartoon came to be a full-size preparatory model of the whole. This meant that the entire composition would be worked out in detail on paper, until the artist was satisfied that the only element missing was color. In larger undertakings the artist might involve himself only up through this stage, and leave the transfer of the cartoon to the wall and the execution in paint to assistants.[36]

This new procedure was of great significance. Perhaps most important of all, it stimulated a reconsideration of the role of drawing in the creation of a painting. If, until then, drawing had been regarded as little more than a link between the artistic conception and the finished product, it now came to be looked on as possessing a significance of its own, and as constituting a point of arrival in its own right. At first restricted to the cartoon, this notion was eventually extended to any creative drawing. In the second edition of his *Lives*, Vasari coined a definition expressive of the new attitude. He applied to the medium of drawing a notion first formulated by the ancient Greeks: that the work of·art materializes a form pre-existing in the mind of the artist.[37] Drawing, he implied, is the stage at which this materialization takes place, and a drawing is nothing less than a visible expression of the concept formed in the mind: "One may conclude that this drawing is nothing but a visible expression and declaration of the concept which one has in the mind" [. . . si può conchiudere che esso disegno altro non sia che una apparente espressione e dichiarazione del concetto che si ha nell'animo. . . .].[38]

The reconsideration of drawing was given a further impetus by a particular development in the technique of drawing on paper. Until the later Quattrocento, as Gombrich pointed out, "it remains remarkable how rare even small *pentimenti* are in drawings. As a rule, if one of these artists did have doubts about which pattern to adopt for a composition, he preferred to begin afresh, to draw two or more alternatives side by side."[39]

It was given to Leonardo da Vinci to liberate drawing from such inhibitions. The method Leonardo devised consists in first laying down the components of a composition without insisting on their definition: "Sketch subject pictures quickly and do not give the limbs too much finish; [only] indicate their position."[40] The draftsman was then to adjust and correct the forms again and again with *pentimenti* until the desired outline was finally chosen. This was truly a new exploitation of the drawing medium, whereby the working creativity of the mind was registered more spontaneously.

Leonardo was well aware of the revolutionary character of his method and he justified it by comparing it with the poet's working method: "Now have you never thought about how poets compose their verse? They do not trouble to trace beautiful letters nor do they mind crossing out several lines so as to make them better."[41] Expressed at a time when painting was struggling for recognition among the liberal arts, such remarks must have encouraged recognition of the potential connections between artistic creativity and the drawing medium.[42] Along with the new method itself, they would also have easily stimulated in the contemporaries a new curiosity about drawings.

Chiefly as a result of these developments, drawings in the sixteenth century acquired a new status: their association with creativity and with artistic genius became openly recognized and they enjoyed a new level of appreciation. The drawings of the greater artists became particularly sought after. Pietro Aretino's request to Michelangelo is an illuminating testimony to the value that could be attached to them: "But why, my Lord, do you not reward this great devotion of mine—I who bow to your celestial qualities—with a relic of these sheets that are less precious to you? Certainly I would appreciate two traces of charcoal on a sheet more than so many goblets and chains which this and that prince ever offers me." [Ma perchè, o Signore, non remunerate voi la cotanta divozione di me, che inchino le celesti qualità di voi, con una reliquia di quelle carte, che vi son meno care? Certo che apprezzerei due segni di carbone in un foglio più, che quante coppe e catene mi presentò mai questo principe, e quello].[43] Drawings, indeed, came to be valued not only aesthetically, but for what they might disclose about the artistic personality of the artist. More specifically, they would be scrutinized for aspects which the finished works might not reveal, and in this the drawing decisively took on the value of complement to the finished work. In some cases an artist's drawings could even be judged of more aesthetic merit than his paintings, as in the case of Vasari's estimate of Giulio Romano: "One could affirm that Giulio always expressed his concepts better in drawings than in the execution or in paintings, for in the former one can see more vivacity, vigour and feeling." [si può affermare che Giulio esprimesse sempre meglio i suoi concetti ne'disegni che nell'operare o nelle pitture, vedendosi in quelli più vivacità, fierezza ed affetto.].[44]

A logical consequence of the new interest in drawings was that they came to be collected on a systematic basis, in a spirit that has continued to the present day. If until then they had been preserved mostly as study material or as objects of curiosity, they now began to be gathered for historical purposes, and the ground was laid for a wholly self-sufficient field of connoisseurship and aesthetic satisfaction. Giorgio Vasari was the first collector of drawings in the modern sense. His *Libro de' Disegni*, meant as a graphic illustration to his *Lives*, was the first compilation of drawings that aimed at the new ideal.[45] Included in it were specimens by artists ranging from Cimabue to his own contemporaries. This exhibition presents two drawings that were originally part of Vasari's collection (cat. nos. D5, D25). It is further testimony of the new status drawings had achieved that Vasari framed the great majority in his *Libro* with highly decorative, individually conceived borders.

The Practical Importance of Drawing

Drawing, in sixteenth century Florence, played a major role in nearly all the visual arts. It was the most common means of giving birth to a project and of developing it, often as far as its final configuration. The convenience of its handling had also established it as the most natural visual means of communication between the patron and the artist, especially when distance separated them. For these reasons alone, draftsmanship was a primary requirement for any serious aspiring artist.

The Quattrocento had already acknowledged the importance of the discipline of drawing, especially for the painter, the sculptor, and the architect. Ghiberti, for instance, had declared it the most determining condition of excellence for both the painter and the sculptor: "the more accomplished he will be [in drawing], the more perfect will be the sculptor, and likewise the painter" [quanto sarà più perito [nel disegno], tanto sarà perfettissimo lo scultore e cosi il pittore].[46] Filarete had similarly recognized it as a necessity for the architect: "he needs to know the art of drawing" [bisognia che sappia l'arte del disegnio].[47].

The mid-sixteenth century Florentine attitude towards the medium was basically a continuation and a deepening of these ideas. In the section which he added at the beginning of *Della Pittura* in the second edition of his *Lives*, Vasari attempted to codify the prevailing current notion by demonstrating that *disegno*, understood as the discipline of drawing, was truly the key to success in all three arts.

Vasari began by pointing out that the hand must be trained so as to materialize, in drawing, the concepts already existing in the artist's mind: "But be as it may, this *disegno* needs, when it extracts from the judgment the invention of a certain thing, that the hand, through many years of study and practice, be swift and apt to draw and correctly express whatever nature has created, with pen, stylus, charcoal, pencil or other thing; because, when the intellect correctly sends out refined concepts, these hands that have practiced drawing for many years make known the perfection and excellence of the arts together with the knowledge of the artist." [Ma sia come si voglia, questo disegno ha bisogno, quando cava l'invenzione d'una qualche cosa dal giudizio, che la mano sia, mediante lo studio ed esercizio di molti anni, spedita ed atta a disegnare ed esprimere bene qualunque cosa ha la natura creata, con penna, con stile, con carbone, con matita o con altra cosa: perchè, quando l'intelletto manda fuori i concetti purgati e con giudizio, fanno quelle mani che hanno molti anni esercito il disegno, conoscere la perfezione ed eccellenza dell'arti, ed il sapere dell'-artefice insieme][48]. But Vasari was also acquainted with sculptors who were not too proficient in drawing, primarily through lack of practice, and yet who could work in sculpture rather well. He therefore added—somewhat to the detriment of the theory he was interested in building up—that a sculptor *can* give excellent embodiment to his artistic concepts without recourse to drawing: "And since some sculptors at times do not have much practice in lines and contours, consequently they cannot draw on paper; these, in exchange, with beautiful proportion and measure, making, with earth or wax, men, animals and other things in relief, do the same as does the one who draws on paper or other flat surfaces perfectly." [E perchè alcuni scultori talvolta non hanno molto pratica nelle linee e ne'dintorni, onde non possono disegnare in carta: eglino, in quel cambio, con bella proporzione e misura facendo con terra o cera uomini, animali ed altre cose di rilievo, fanno il medesimo che fa colui, il quale perfettamente disegna in carta o in su altri piani].[49]

After enumerating the different types of drawing, Vasari then proceeded to describe the value that drawing could be to each one of the three arts. The aspect he focused on, and through which he correlated all three, was, understandably, the outline. For architecture this was easily established "because its *disegni* are composed only of lines; which so far as the architect is concerned are nothing but the beginning and end of his art, since the rest, with the aid of wooden models taken from the said lines, is nothing but the work of carvers and bricklayers" [perciocchè i disegni di quella non son composti se non di linee: il che non è altro, quanto all'architettore, che il principio e la fine di quell' arte, perchè il restante, mediante i modelli di legname tratti dalle dette linee, non è altro che opera de scarpellini e muratori].[50] Sculpture was then treated: "in sculpture the drawing of all the contours is of use, because the sculptor uses it in going around from view to view. . . ." [nella scultura serve il disegno di tutti i contorni, perchè a veduta per veduta se ne serve lo scultore. . . .][51]. Painting was likewise treated, with the outlines as the focal point: "In painting, the line-drawings are useful in many ways, but particularly to outline every figure. . . ."

[Nella pittura servono i lineamenti in piu modi, ma particolarmente a dintornare ogni figura. . . .][52] Then came the conclusive statement: "Hence it follows that whoever understands and manages these lines correctly will be, with the aid of practice and judgment, most excellent in each one of these arts." [E di qui nasce, che chiunque intende e maneggia bene queste linee, sarà in ciascuna di queste arti, mediante la pratica ed il giudizio, eccellentissimo].[53] Thus had *disegno,* understood as the discipline of drawing, been established as the key to success in all three arts.[54]

It is especially for the painter that drawing was most relevant, and Vasari came back to this idea repeatedly. Perhaps his most determined justification can be seen in his life of Titian. Expanding on what he had written on the subject at the beginning of *Della Pittura,* Vasari specified drawing as a necessity for the clarification of the *invenzioni,* since the mind cannot imagine them perfectly but needs their externalizing: "for him who wants to dispose his compositions and establish his inventions well, it is necessary that he should first lay them out on paper in different fashions, in order to see how the whole works out together. For the reason that the "idea" cannot see nor imagine the inventions perfectly within herself, if she does not reveal and show her concept to the eyes of the body so that the latter may help her to form a good judgment" [è necessario a chi vuol bene disporre i componimenti ed accomodare l'invenzioni, ch'e'fa bisogno prima in più modi differenti porle in carta, per vedere come il tutto torna insieme. Conciosiachè l'idea non può vedere nè immaginare perfettamente in se stessa l'invenzioni, se non apre e non mostra il suo concetto agli occhi corporali che l'aiutino a farne buon giudizio][55]. The practice of drawing is also judged to fill the mind with beautiful artistic concepts: "Drawing on paper will fill the mind with beautiful concepts" [disegnando in carta, si viene a empiere la mente di bei concetti].[56]. Drawing will also enable the artist to learn how to depict the objects of nature without needing them in front of him: "Drawing on paper . . . one learns to depict all the things in nature from memory, without needing to have them constantly before one's eyes" [disegnando in carta . . . s'impara a fare a mente tutte le cose della natura, senza avere a tenerle sempre dinanzi].[57] Vasari also held drawing to be invaluable for developing facility, ease, and judgment: "when one has formed one's hand by drawing on paper, one comes little by little to execute one's works in drawing and painting with greater ease; and so by practicing the art, one makes one's manner and judgment perfect, doing away with the labour and effort with which are executed the paintings" [quando altri ha fatto la mano disegnando in carta, si vien poi di mano in mano con più agevolezza a mettere in opera disegnando e dipignendo: e così facendo pratica nell'arte, si fa la maniera ed il giudizio perfetto, levando via quella fatica e stento con che si conducono le pitture.][58] Vasari likewise considered drawing essential to acquire command over the human figure: "one needs to give a great deal of study to the nudes, if one wishes to understand them well; which does not happen, nor is it possible, without laying them out on paper." [bisogna fare grande studio sopra gl'ignudi a volergli intender bene; il che non vien fatto, nè si può, senza mettere in carta].[59] It is, finally, in the repeated drawing of selected antique or modern works that the artist will learn how to endow natural forms with a degree of perfection not usually found in nature: "He who has not drawn much, nor studied selected antique or modern things, cannot work well from memory by himself; nor can he improve the things that are depicted from life by giving them that grace and perfection which art gives beyond the order of nature, since the latter ordinarily does some parts that are not beautiful" [chi non ha disegnato assai, e studiato cose scelte antiche o moderne, non può fare bene di pratica da sè nè aiutare le cose che si ritranno dal vivo, dando loro quella grazia e perfezione che dà l'arte fuori dell'ordine della natura, la quale fa ordinariamente alcune parti che non son belle][60].

Such an all-out attempt to justify drawing arose out of Vasari's disapproval of Giorgione for having initiated the method of developing a painting with the brush directly on canvas, without the required drawing stages.[61] The typical Florentine method in Vasari's day had, on the contrary, remained essentially the same as that popularized in Rome and Florence during Raphael's lifetime: from its first intimation in the artist's mind, the concept would be evolved graphically on paper until its full clarification (to the exclusion of color) in the cartoon.

The first stage of this method[62] "consisted of *schizzi*, or rough compositional sketches. Vasari described them as follows: "One makes them to find the manner of the attitudes, and the first composition of the work; they are made in the form of a blotch, and laid out by us only as a rough draft of the whole." [si fanno per trovar il modo delle attitudini, ed il primo componimento dell'opra; e sono fatti in forma di una macchia, ed accennati solamente da noi in una sola bozza del tutto].[63] A satisfactory composition of the whole having been arrived at (e.g. cat. no. D43), the artist would proceed to the second stage—although, needless to say, at all times was he liable to make drastic revisions. Here he might study specific aspects, such as the fall of light, or the grouping of a certain number of figures (e.g., cat. no. D18). He would also make individual studies of poses that gave him difficulty (e.g. cat. nos. D2 and D41). He might even wish to draw the whole figure composition in the nude so as to realize the anatomies with greater clarity (cat. no. D30). Unlike the practice in Raphael's time, when the artist would normally work assiduously from the model, the mid-century artist would, ideally, work from his own knowledge; but he might draw from life if (in Vasari's own words) he did not feel secure enough.[64]

The third stage began with the layout of the whole in as finished a form as desired. This drawing would then be squared (see, for instance cat. nos. D48 and D40) and its content would be transferred to the cartoon, at the dimensions of the painting-to-be. Then, applying the cartoon to the surface to be painted, the artist would go over the outlines with an iron stylus so as to imprint them. This accomplished, the cartoon would be set up next to the area to be painted, and the artist would proceed to paint, closely following the distribution of light and shade embodied in the cartoon. As mentioned earlier, in larger undertakings the master might entrust the transfer of the cartoon and the execution in paint to assistants. In this case he would dictate the coloring and merely exercise supervision. The decoration of the Palazzo Vecchio by Vasari witnessed this procedure.

As should be expected, it is essentially around drawing that the education of the Florentine painter revolved, and copying was the first requirement. Among the antique works which he would have drawn were statues and architectural ornaments, but especially reliefs on both sarcophagi and arches.[65] Chief among the modern works which he was expected to copy were those of Michelangelo, including his cartoon for the *Battle of Cascina*. The present exhibition includes a copy by Rosso Fiorentino (cat. no. D8) of Michelangelo's *Apollo* in the Bargello (Florence). Another important cartoon for copying, of which this exhibition offers a version (by Vasari himself; cat. no. D31), was the one for the *Martyrdom of the Ten Thousand* by Perino del Vaga. Vasari gives us an interesting glimpse into the role of drawing in the formation of the painter when telling about his trip to Rome with Francesco Salviati. They set out to draw all the significant works available, and to facilitate this coverage they divided them between themselves; their evenings were partly spent making sketches of each other's copies.

Disegno and the Formal Content of Painting

We saw earlier that possession of *disegno*, for the painter, referred primarily to his command over the composition of the individual human figure. It is first and foremost as the gradual perfection of this command that Vasari saw the history of painting to his own day.[66]. He indeed conceived of *disegno* thus understood as an ability which, having all but died out at the fall of the Roman Empire, was fully revived by Giotto and brought to perfection in the works of Michelangelo.

When Vasari's conception of the history of painting appeared in the first edition of his *Lives* (in 1550), the achievements of Michelangelo in the composition of the human figure had already affected the course of Florentine painting radically. They had first of all contributed to establishing the human figure, especially the nude figure, as the central subject of painting. And this is indeed of itself an important characteristic of mid-sixteenth century Florentine painting. Secondly, they had contributed to establishing the composition of the figure as the major challenge and the foremost preoccupation of the painter. The more varied and complicated the poses, the more the artist would reveal his command of the human figure, and therefore the more he could claim the praise of his fellow citizens. In this challenge and in this preoccupation resides perhaps the single most comprehensive explanation of the contorted poses, the crowding of bodies, and the seemingly irrelevant display of muscular figures in the painting of the period. The three major contemporary examples from which the painter derived these interests were all Michelangelo's works: the cartoon for the *Battle of Cascina*, the *Sistine Ceiling*, and the *Last Judgment*.

If we now turn to the repercussions that *disegno* (with more inclusive connotations) had on the Florentine attitude towards color, we find that in Vasari, for instance, there was, theoretically at least, no lack of interest in it. Color was recognized as the area where painting proved itself decisively superior to sculpture in its ability to materialize the transient phenomena of nature, the textural quality of human flesh . . . etc.[67] Vasari had, in fact, the highest respect for the coloring of artists like Correggio and Titian, and he admitted that the complete perfection of painting involved the perfection of both *disegno* and *colorire*. But he also recognized that such a perfection was very rarely attainable: "This art is so difficult and has so many main branches, that very often an artist is not able to practice them all to perfection. For there have been many who have drawn divinely, but have shown some imperfection in coloring; others have been marvelous in coloring, but have not drawn half as well." [È quest'arte tanto difficile ed ha tanti capi, che uno artefice bene spesso non li può tutti fare perfettamente; perchè molti sono che hanno disegnato divinamente, e nel colorire hanno avuto qualche imperfezione; altri hanno colorito maravigliosamente, e non hanno disegnato alla metà].[68] And he added that these difficulties were partly due to training, which might lead one painter to specialize from youth in *disegno* and another to concentrate on color: "All this arises from judgment and from the practice which is taken in youth: for one it will be in *disegno*, and for another it will be in color." [Questo nascie tutto dal giudizio e da una pratica che si piglia da giovane, chi nel disegno e chi sopra i colori].[69]

Since the education of the Florentine artist centered on *disegno*, it was to be expected that his handling of color should not as a rule reach that perfection which Vasari had in mind. The very method of preparing and evolving a painting, and the belief that it was in qualities of draftsmanship that the core of artistic excellence lay, also predisposed him to a lesser interest in color. And this predisposition partly explains the relatively dry coloring of the painting of the period. On the other hand, an artist of exceptional stature like Salviati could occasionally rise to levels of coloring decidedly superior. The rich, vibrating chiaroscuro of his frescoes in the Oratorio of San Giovanni Decollato in Rome demonstrates this very clearly.[70] But the more normal Florentine color quality of the period should not be seen exclusively in negative terms: the linear content of Florentine painting was positively motivated as well, and moreover we shall now see how both linearity and color were really complementary to one another.

The essentially linear treatment of form had been common to pre-High Renaissance painting as a whole, and it is a commonplace to say that Leonardo brought about a revolution in this domain with his *sfumato*. His motivations had been, among others, partly naturalistic (integration of the forms in air and atmosphere) and partly logical (line does not exist in nature and therefore ought to have no place in a painting). This is the attitude which was adopted by artists like Raphael, Fra Bartolommeo, and Correggio. In the *Doni Holy Family*, on the other hand, Michelangelo had resisted Leonardo's innovation and proclaimed the integrity of the outline and the purity of the silhouette.

This linear mode of circumscription found popularity among mid-sixteenth century Florentine painters under the stimulus of a variety of interests. One of the most important of these was the interest in the qualities of antique relief sculpture,[71] and in relief (*rilievo*) in general. It remains true that Leonardo had been no less concerned with *rilievo*, but he had sought to accommodate it mainly to his naturalistic ambitions. In so doing, however, he had caused the painted form to weaken or to lose in strength of pure sculptural presence. It is such a presence that Michelangelo had attempted to recapture in the *Doni Holy Family*, and with which the mid-century artists, following Michelangelo, continued to be preoccupied.

Interest in the technical mastery of the human figure (or in *disegno* thus understood) was equally a major factor in dictating the mid-century attitude towards the outline. For if the ability to compose the human figure (or, one might say, to draw the human figure) constitutes the single most important ambition of the painter, it follows that he ought to avoid anything that would tend to veil or obscure not only this ability, but the structural and plastic values of the figure. Anything, on the other hand, that would bring out this ability and project these values in a more arresting and compelling manner should be exploited. The graphic treatment of form as we find it in the painting of that period does precisely that. The values just mentioned are, in fact, partly dependent on it for their very level of quality. The blurring of the outlines was thus as inimical to Florentine aesthetic ideals as it was to the artist's display of his own command over the human figure. That the latter was of the highest importance is brought home in frequent references. Vasari, for instance, advocated the practice of drawing so that the artist would not be forced "to conceal beneath the loveliness of colors the painful [result] of not knowing how to draw." [avere a nascere sotto la vaghezza de' colori lo stento del non sapere disegnare].[72]

A similar discussion applies to color. In a mid-sixteenth century Florentine painting, color was assigned a very definite role: that of contributing to the formal clarification and articulation of the forms, and to the assertion and projection of their structural and plastic values. But in so doing it was made to take a secondary position and to relinquish the richness which one admires in a Venetian painting.

Deep shadows, particularly, were to be avoided. Just as the contours were forced to stiffen in order to project the structural and plastic values of the figures more eloquently, likewise color was compelled to adopt a more frozen mien in order to render this projection more assertive. Both were really meant to work hand in hand. The most distinguished representative of this sculptural mode of vision operating in Florence was Bronzino. Unusually gifted in color, Bronzino usually succeeded in preserving a purity of atmosphere totally devoid of the dryness one generally finds in his Florentine contemporaries.

Maurice Poirier
[*New York University*]

Notes

1. This essay has been written in the context of a larger study (which will be submitted as a doctoral dissertation) dealing with the concept of *disegno* during the Renaissance and afterwards. I wish to acknowledge my deep indebtedness to Professor Craig Hugh Smyth for his guidance and encouragement. I also wish to express my gratitude to the Samuel H. Kress Foundation for a grant which has made possible the continuation of this research.

2. See the entry for instance in the *Vocabolario degli Accademici della Crusca* (various editions).

3. Among the more important works incorporating discussions on the concept of *disegno* for the period under consideration, the following may be cited: K. Birch-Hirschfeld, *Die Lehre von der Malerei im Cinquecento* (Rome, 1912); E. Panofsky, *Idea*, first publ. 1924, trans. by J. Peake (Columbia, S.C., 1968); L Grassi, *Storia del Disegno* (Rome, 1947); *idem, Il Disegno Italiano dal Trecento al Seicento* (Rome, 1956); and J. Rouchette, *La Renaissance que nous a léguée Vasari* (Paris, 1959). The references in this essay will be kept at a minimum.

4. L. B. Alberti, *Della Pittura*, ed. L. Mallé (Florence, 1950), p. 82. Alberti divided painting into three categories: *circonscriptione, compositione,* and *ricevere di lumi.*

5. *Ibid.,* p. 82.

6. *Ibid.,* p. 87.

7. Piero della Francesca, *De prospectiva pingendi,* ed. N. Fasola (Florence, 1942), p. 63. Piero subdivided painting into *disegno, commensuratio,* and *colorare.*

8. Alberti, *op. cit.,* p. 82.

9. One of the conveniences of this characterization was that it could apply to an architectural construction as well as to a human body. Significantly, Alberti's most ambitious definitions of beauty are found in his architectural treatise, *De Re Aedificatoria.* For example, in Book IX: "Thus we may say that beauty is a certain agreement and harmony of parts within that to which they belong, with regard to a definite number, proportionality and order, such as concinnity (i.e., the absolute and primary law of nature) demands." (Translation taken from Panofsky, *op. cit.,* p. 54). On this subject see especially Panofsky, *idem,* pp. 47ff.

10. Alberti, *op. cit.,* p. 88.

11. P. Pino, *Dialogo di Pittura* (Venice, 1548) in P. Barocchi, *Trattati d'Arte del Cinquecento* (Bari, 1960) I, p. 113.

12. *Ibid.,* p. 114.

13. *Ibid.,* p. 114.

14. *Ibid.,* p. 104. Elsewhere in the text, Pino had defined beauty mainly in terms of proportion: "altro non è bellezza, in ciascuna spezie creata, ch'una commensurazione e corrispondenzia de' membri prodotti dalla natura senza alcuno impedimento de mali accidenti" (p. 98).

15. L. Dolce, *Dialogo della Pittura* (Venice, 1557) in Barocchi, *op. cit.,* I, p. 164.

16. Earlier Dolce had connected proportion and beauty in an uncompromising fashion: "Non procedendo la bellezza da altro, che da una convenevole proporzione che comunemente ha il corpo umano, e particolarmente tra se ogni membro, et il contrario derivando da sproporzione" (*ibid.,* p. 155).

17. *Ibid.,* p. 176.

18. G. Vasari, *Vite,* ed. G. Milanesi (Florence, 1878-1881)—henceforth, in this essay, referred to as Vasari-Milanesi—IV, p. 8. It is true that Vasari, immediately after, discusses beauty of composition in the human figure under *maniera.* But the latter is not the specific constructive process that materializes this beauty of composition. *Maniera* controls what one could call the general style of the artistic creation (and by the same token of the work of art). Under its dependency fall qualities of color and *invenzione* as well as of *disegno.* This is made clear when Vasari says that until the third age *maniera* was still lacking in the following: "la copia de' belli abiti, la varieta di tante bizzarrie, la vaghezza de' colori, la universita ne' casamenti, e la lontananza e varieta ne' paesi" (IV, p. 9). Throughout the *Lives,* indeed, *disegno* irrevocably emerges as the most immediate and comprehensive *régisseur* of compositional qualities in the human figure (to the exclusion of color). On *maniera,* see C. H. Smyth, *Mannerism and Maniera* (New York, 1962).

19. So far, our discussion of *disegno* has been focused on the composition of the single figure. The term could also be used to refer to the linear layout of the painting as a whole. Dolce, for instance, began by defining *disegno* as "la forma con che egli la [invenzione] rappresenta" (*op. cit.,* p. 164). But this application of *disegno* remained secondary at the time, even for Dolce, and it would be inappropriate to carry it along in our discussion. It is interesting to note that F. Baldinucci, a century later, defined the expression *aver disegno* in terms of both aspects: "Aver disegno, termine de Pittori, e vale sapere ordinatamente disporre la 'nvenzione, dopo aver bene e aggiustamente delineata e contornata ogni figura, o altra cosa che si voglia rappresentare" (*Vocabolario Toscano dell' Arte del Disegno,* Florence, 1681, *voce*).

20. Dolce, *op. cit.,* p. 162.

21. G. P. Lomazzo, *Idea del Tempio della Pittura,* first publ. 1590, Colombo ed. (Rome, 1947), p. 71.

22. It is worth noting that the fifteenth century architect Filarete occasionally referred to the architectural model as a *disegnio rilevato* or a *disegnio di legname* (A. Filarete, *Trattato di Architettura,* ed. as *Filarete's Treatise on Architecture* by J. Spencer (New Haven, 1965), II, folio 8r). The

significance of this use of *disegno* cannot be discussed here.

23. L. B. Alberti, *De Re Aedificatoria,* trans. by C. Bartoli (Florence, 1550), Book I, p. 9.

24. Vasari-Milanesi, I, p. 275.

25. *Ibid.,* I, p. 136.

26. Leonardo, *Trattato,* ed. H. Ludwig, in *Quellenschriften für Kunstgeschichte,* XV, (Vienna, 1882), 39, p. 86.

27. A. Bronzino, *Letter to Varchi* in Barocchi, *op. cit.,* I, p. 67.

28. Vasari-Milanesi, VII, p. 151.

29. F. da Sangallo, *Letter to Varchi* in Barocchi, *op. cit.,* I, p. 73.

30. V. Danti, *Il primo libro del trattato delle perfette proporzioni* (Florence, 1567) in Barocchi, *op. cit.,* I, p. 236.

31. Sangallo, *op. cit.,* p. 73.

32. E.g. in Vasari-Milanesi, I, p. 9.

33. On this *Accademia,* see N. Pevsner, *Academies of Art, Past and Present* (Cambridge, 1940), pp. 42ff.

34. As quoted by Pevsner, *op. cit.,* p. 296.

35. The views on this subject vary. See for instance M. Meiss and L. Tintori, *The Painting of the Life of St. Francis in Assisi* (New York, 1962), pp. 3ff. and R. Oertel "Wandmalerei und Zeichnung in Italien: Die Anfänge der Entwurfszeichnung und ihre monumentalen Vorstufen," *Mitteilungen des Kunsthistorischen Instituts in Florenz,* V, 1940, pp. 217ff. The latest study of this problem is by B. Degenhart and A. Schmitt, *Corpus der italienischen Zeichnungen 1300-1450* (Berlin, 1968), I, part 1, pp. xiii ff.

36. This came to be a practice especially of Raphael and his circle.

37. On this notion in Antiquity, see Panofsky, *op. cit.,* pp. 27ff.

38. Vasari-Milanesi, I, p 168. Vasari's definition, expressed in 1568, also reflects the contemporary interest in clarifying the process of conception of the work of art. Already in 1549, in a book entitled *Disegno* (publ. in Venice), A. Doni had stated that "il disegno non è altro che speculatione divina che produce un'arte eccelentissima, talmente che tu non puoi operare cosa nessuna nella scultura, e nella pittura senza la guida di questa speculatione e disegno" (p. 7v). This subject, which is more suitably handled in the context of late sixteenth century theory, cannot be gone into here.

39. E. Gombrich, "Leonardo's Method for Working out Compositions" in *Norm and Form* (London, 1966), p. 59.

40. Quoted by Gombrich, *op. cit.,* p. 60, from Leonardo's *Treatise on Painting.*

41. *Ibid.,* p. 59.

42. This was originally suggested to me by a passage in Prof. Smyth's book, *op. cit.,* p. 77, note 168.

43. In G. Bottari, ed., *Raccolta di Lettere* (Rome, 1759), III, p. 77.

44. Vasari-Milanesi, V, p. 528.

45. On Vasari's collection of drawings, see especially O. Kurz, "Giorgio Vasari's 'Libro de' Disegni'," *Old Master Drawings,* nos. 45 and 47, June and Dec. 1937, pp. 1ff. and pp. 32ff. See also the exhibition catalogue: *Giorgio Vasari Dessinateur et Collectionneur,* Cabinet des Dessins, Louvre, Paris, 1965.

46. L. Ghiberti, *I Commentari,* ed. O. Morisani (Naples, 1947), p. 5.

47. Filarete, *op. cit.,* II, folio 113r.

48. Vasari-Milanesi, I, p. 169.

49. *Ibid.,* p. 169.

50. *Ibid.,* p. 170.

51. *Ibid.,* p. 170.

52. *Ibid.,* p. 170.

53. *Ibid.,* p. 170.

54. It is interesting to note that even within the Florentine *ambiente,* there were views at odds with this notion. Cellini, for instance, insisted that sculpture was the key to success in both painting and architecture (let alone in its own field): "La scultura è madre di tutte l'arte dove si interviene disegno, e quello che sara valente scultore e di buona maniera, gli sara facilissimo l'esser buon prospettivo e architeto e maggior pittor, che quegli che non posseggono la scultura" (*Letter to Varchi* in Barocchi, *op. cit.,* I, p. 81).

55. Vasari-Milanesi, VII, p. 427.

56. *Ibid.,* p. 427.

57. *Ibid.,* p. 427.

58. *Ibid.,* p. 427.

59. *Ibid.,* p. 427.

60. *Ibid.,* p. 447. Vasari and his contemporaries considered it the task of the painter to improve upon the forms of nature. This problem is beyond the scope of the present study.

61. A very good discussion of the Venetian approach, with the relevant bibliography, is given by D. Rosand, *Palma Giovane and Venetian Mannerism,* unpubl. dissertation, Columbia Univ., 1965, pp. 17ff.

62. A discussion of this method is provided in C. de Tolnay, *History and Technique of Old Master Drawings* (New York, 1943), pp. 19ff.

63. Vasari-Milanesi, I, p. 174.

64. *Ibid.,* p. 174. This practice was intimately connected with the belief that the artist's task was to improve upon the forms of nature.

65. On the importance of antique reliefs, see especially Smyth, *op. cit., passim.*

66. This subject is treated in S. L. Alpers, "*Ekphrasis* and Aesthetic Attitudes in Vasari's *Lives,*" *Journal of the Warburg and Courtauld Institutes,* XXIII, 1960, pp. 190ff.

67. See especially his letter to Varchi, in Barocchi, *op. cit.,* I, p. 61.

68. Vasari-Milanesi, IV, p. 113. Pino had recognized that a perfect painter would combine Michelangelo's *disegno* with the coloring of Titian (*op. cit.,* p. 127).

69. *Ibid.,* p. 113.

70. The superiority of Salviati in the handling of color was recognized by Vasari, *ibid.,* VII, p. 41.

71. On this subject, see Smyth, *op. cit., passim.*

72. Vasari-Milanesi, VII, p. 427.

Drawings

Selected Bibliography

F. Antal, "Drawings by Salviati and Vasari after a Lost Picture by Rosso," *Old Master Drawings*, Sept./March, 1939/40, pp. 47-49.

R. Bacou and C. Monbeig-Goguel, *Giorgio Vasari—Dessinateur et Collectionneur*, Paris, Cabinet des Dessine, Louvre, 1965.

P. Barocchi, *Il Vasari Pittore*, Milan, 1964.

P. Barocchi, *Complementi al Vasari Pittore, Atti del'Accademia Toscana-di Scienze e Lettere La Colombania*, Florence, 1963-1964, pp. 253-309.

P. Barocchi, *Mostra di Disegni del Vasari e della Sua Cerchia*, Gabinetto Disegni e Stampe degli Uffizi, 1964.

J. Bean and F. Stampfle, *Drawings from New York Collections—I—The Italian Renaissance*, Greenwich, 1965.

O. Benesch, *Master Drawings in the Albertina*, Vienna, 1967.

M. Benisovich, "The Drawings of Stradanus (Jan Van der Straeten) in the Cooper Union Museum for the Arts of Decoration, New York," *The Art Bulletin*, Vol. 38, Dec. 1965, pp. 249-253.

B. Berenson, *The Drawings of the Florentine Painters*, Chicago, 1938, 3 Vols.

R. Borghini, *Il Riposo*, Florence, 1584.

P. Cannon Brookes, "Three Notes on Maso da San Friano," *Burlington Magazine*, Vol. 108, April 1965, pp. 192-197.

W. R. Carden, *The Life of Giorgio Vasari. A Study of the Later Renaissance in Italy*, London, 1910.

E. A. Carroll, "Some Drawings by Rosso Fiorentino," *Burlington Magazine*, Vol. 103, Nov. 1961, pp. 446-454.

B. F. Davidson, "Vasari's Deposition in Arezzo," *The Art Bulletin*, XXXVI, Sept. 1954, pp. 228-231.

B. F. Davidson, *Mostra di Disegni di Perino del Vaga e la Sua Cerchia*, Gabinetto Disegni e Stampe degli Uffizi, 1966.

S. Freedberg. *Parmigianino, His Works in Painting*, Cambridge, Mass., 1950.

K. Frey, *Der literarische Nachlass Giorgio Vasari*, Munich, Vol. I, 1923, Vol. II, 1930.

H. W. Frey, *Neue Briefe von Giorgio Vasari*, Munich, 1940.

D. Heikamp, "A Florence la maison de Vasari," *L'oeil*, Vol. 137, May 1966. pp. 2-9.

F. Kossoff, "Lelio Orsi and The Walk to Emmaus," *Master Drawings*, Vol. IV/no. 4, 1966, pp. 415-418.

O. Kurz, "Giorgio Vasari 'Libro dei Disegni," *Old Master Drawings*, XII, 1937, p. 32.

F. Lugt, *Les Marques de Collections de dessins et d'estampes . . .* , Amsterdam, 1921.

F. Lugt, *Les Marques de Collections de dessins et d'estampes . . . Supplément*, The Hague, 1956.

A. Mongan and P. Sachs, *Drawings in the Fogg Museum of Art*, Cambridge, Mass., 1946.

A. Mongan, ed., *One Hundred Master Drawings*, Cambridge, Mass., 1949.

E. Pillsbury, "Drawings by Vasari and Vincenzo Borghini for the 'Apparato' in Florence in 1565," *Master Drawings* Vol. V/no. 3, 1967, pp. 281-283.

A. E. Popham, "The Drawings of Girolamo Bedoli," *Master Drawings,* Vol. II/no. 3, 1964, pp. 243-267.

A. E. Popham and K. M. Fenwick, *European Drawings in the Collection of The National Gallery of Canada,* Toronto, 1965.

W. Prinz, *Vasaris Sammlung von Künstlerbildnissen,* Florence, 1966.

T. C. Rearick, *The Drawings of Pontormo,* Cambridge, 1964, 2 Vols.

J. Schulz, "Vasari at Venice," *Burlington Magazine,* Vol. 103, 1961, pp. 500-511.

U. Scoti-Bertinelli, *Giorgio Vasari Scrittore,* Pisa, 1905.

F. Stampfle, "A Ceiling Design by Vasari," *Master Drawings,* Vol. 6/no. 3, 1968, pp. 266-271.

W. Stechow, "An Altarpiece by Vasari," *Art Quarterly,* Vol. 2, 1939, pp. 178-184.

G. Thiem, "Vasaris Entwürfe für die Gemälde in der Sala Grande des Palazzo Vecchio zu Florenz,"*Zeitschrift für Kunstgeschichte,* XXIV, 1960, pp,

G. Thiem, "Neuentdeckte Zeichnungen Vasaris und Naldinis für die Sala Grande des Palazzo Vecchio in Florenz," *Zeitschrift für Kunstgeschichte,* 1968, pp. pp. 143-150.

U. Thieme and F. Becker. *Allgemeines Lexikon der Bildenden Künstler,* Leipzig, 1907-1947.

A. Venturi, *Storia dell'Arte Italiana—La Pittura del Cinquecento,* parte VI, Milan, 1933, Vol. XI.

F. Viatte, "Two Studies by Naldini for the 'Deposition' in S. Simone, Florence," *Master Drawings,* Vol. V/no. 4, 1967, pp. 384-386.

A. del Vita (Editor), "Le Ricordanze di Giorgio Vasari," Arezzo, 1929.

W. Vitzthum, Paola Barocchi, "Vasari Pittore; Complementi al Vasari Pittore; Mostra dei disegni del Vasari e della Sua Cerchia," *Master Drawings,* 1965, III, no. 1, p. 54.

H. Voss, *Die Malerei der Spätrenaissance in Rom und Florenz,* Berlin, 1920, 2 Vols.

P. Ward-Jackson, *"Vasari the Critic,"* Apollo, Vol. 77, 1963, pp. 454-459.

A. Wyatt, "Le 'Libro dei Disegni 'du Vasari," *Gazette des Beaux-Arts,* 1859, pp. 338-351.

Exhibition Catalogues

Detroit Institute of Arts, *Master Drawings of the Italian Renaissance,* 1960.

Fogg Art Museum, Harvard University, Cambridge, *Anxiety and Elegance. The Human Figure in Italian Art, 1520-1580,* 1962.

Hamburg, Kunsthalle/Cologne, Wallraf-Richartz Museum, *Italienische Meisterzeichnungen vom 14.bis zum 18. Jahrhundert aus amerikanischem Besitz. Die Sammlung Janos Scholz, New York,* 1950.

Indiana University Art Center, Bloomington, *Drawings of the Italian Renaissance From the Scholz Collection,* 1963.

John Herron Art Museum, Indianapolis, *Pontormo to Greco—The Age of Mannerism,* 1954.

The Metropolitan Museum of Art, The Pierpont Morgan Library, *Drawings from New York Collections—I—The Italian Renaissance,* New York, 1965.

Mills College Art Gallery, Oakland, *Drawings from Tuscany and Umbria, 1350-1700,* 1961.

The Newark Museum, *Old Master Drawings,* 1960.

University of Notre Dame Art Gallery, *The Life of the Virgin Mary from the Janos Scholz Collection,* 1967.

Yale University Art Gallery, New Haven, *Italian Drawings from the Collection of Janos Scholz,* 1964.

NICCOLÒ DELL 'ABBATE
(Modena 1512-Fontainebleau 1571)

D1. *Allegory of Peace*

Black chalk heightened with white on grey paper; 9 3/4 x 5 1/2 inches
Lent by a Private Collector, New York
Exhibitions: *Pontormo to Greco—The Age of Mannerism,* John Herron Museum of Art, Indianapolis, Ind., 1954, no. 26, repr.; The Metropolitan Museum of Art, *Drawings from New York Collections—I—The Italian Renaissance,* Nov. 8, 1965-Jan 9, 1966, no. 107, repr.
Bibliography: Jacob Bean and Felice Stampfle, *Drawings from New York Collections—I—The Italian Renaissance,* Greenwich, New York Graphic Society, 1965, no. 107, repr.
Dated in the 1540's, this drawing is characteristic of Niccolò's style before he went to Fontainebleau in 1552. Like Vasari and Bedoli, Niccolò was deeply influenced by Parmigianino. Demonstrating much of the same delicacy and sensitivity of a Parmigianino drawing, Niccolò depicts a triumphant *Peace* standing on the arms of war. Her right arm is raised holding a laurel branch and her head is crowned with laurel leaves. Her robust but graceful form is betrayed by thin, clinging, diaphanous draperies. With a delicacy and refinement, Niccolò applied white highlights to the black drawing.
The drawing is similar to Parmigianino's "Virgins" in the Church of the Steccata, Parma, (reproduced in S. Freedberg, *Parmigianino, His Works in Painting,* Cambridge, 1950, ill. 87) as well as a figure in the Virgilia of the Albertina's drawing *Coriolanus Receiving His Wife and His Mother in the Volscian Camp* (Inv. 14396, reproduced in O. Benesch, *Meisterzeichnungen der Albertina,* 1964, pl. 34). It may have been a study for the decoration of a processional ceremony or for one of Niccolò's frescoes in Modena or Bologna.

ALESSANDRO ALLORI
(Florence 1535-Florence 1607)

D2. *Study of Seated Male Figure* (study for the *Pearl Divers, Studiolo of Francesco I,* Palazzo Vecchio, Florence), ca. 1570-1572

Black crayon on cream paper; 10 3/4 x 7 1/2 inches
Lent by the Pennsylvania Academy of the Fine Arts Collection, on permanent deposit at the Philadelphia Museum of Art
Provenance: Richard Cosway (Lugt 628); Barry Delany (Lugt 350)
Inscriptions: Inscribed in old hand in sepia, verso: ". . . [*A.A.*(?)]*Bronzini*";
Watermark: IHS suspended from cross on trefoil. Formerly attributed to Agnolo Bronzino, the drawing is a study by Bronzino's pupil, Alessandro Allori for the *Pearl Divers* (no. D2a) in the *'Studiolo' of Francesco I,* Palazzo Vecchio, Flor-

ence. The drawing is for a figure in the upper right of the composition. The figure is one of the two inactive but interested spectators who are watching the mass of diving, climbing, and swimming pearl divers.
The drawing was probably one of the several studies for the painting. The Florentine artist often created a rapid sketch (the *schizzo*) of the entire composition and later developed individual elements such as the study exhibited here. Later the cartoon of the entire surface was constructed from these individual elements.
Even though Allori followed closely in the footsteps of Bronzino many of the figures in the *Pearl Divers* are derived from Michelangelo types. The figure climbing onto the rocks to the left of the two spectators is clearly inspired by Michelangelo's *Battle of Cascina* (probably from other copies of Michelangelo's influential cartoon).

BARTOLOMMEO AMMANNATI
(Settignano 1511-Florence 1592)

D3. *River God* (recto); *Sketches for the Finishing of the Vestibule of the Laurenziana, Florence* (verso)

Red chalk and brown ink; 9 5/8 x 7 1/4 inches
Lent by Mr. Harry G. Sperling
Provenance: Giuseppe Vallardi, Milan (Lugt 1223)
Bartolommeo Ammannati was one of the principal Florentine sculptors of Vasari's era. Ammannati worked with Vasari on several occasions, beginning as early as the mid 1530's. Vasari records in Bartolomeo Genga's "Life," that the younger Genga made the friendship of Vasari and Ammannati, and learned much from the sculptor Ammannati (*Lives,* III, p. 266).
Ammannati's greatest achievement was the "Neptune Fountain" that stood in front of the Palazzo Vecchio. Finished in 1571 wih the aid of the Flemish sculptor, Giovanni da Bologna, the drawing, here exhibited, was thought to be a study for one of the figures on this Fountain (Ludwig Goldscheider in a letter to Harry Sperling). Goldscheider later found that the drawing corresponded more closely to two small bronzes by Ammannati in the Bargello, Florence (reproduced in A. E. Popp, *Die Medici Kappelle Michelangelos,* 1922, pls. 78 and 80). There are several possible sources of inspiration for this drawing. Mr. Sperling has brought to my attention a 'river god' in the first floor stucco ceiling design of the Palazzo Firenze, Rome, which corresponds in detail to this drawing. Ammannati could have made this preparatory drawing while in Rome and before going to Florence. We should, also, not overlook Michelangelo's terra cotta 'river gods' for the Medici Chapel. They were to have an influence on the Florentines and it is very likely that Ammannati was not the exception. Nor can we overlook the 'river god' in Marcantonio Raimondi's engraving

after Raphael's drawing of *The Judgment of Paris*. Ammannati's drawing is very close to the Raimondi 'river god!' The basic difference, is that the Ammannati 'river god' is in reverse.

The image of the 'river god' was to be the most popular motif in 16th century Florentine art. The 'river god' is readily recognizable in a great number of contexts.

This drawing is a fine illustration of Vasari's statement that some sculptors, though not good draughtsmen, were good sculptors. Like many of the drawings of Baccio Bandinelli, Ammannati's drawing does not demonstrate the same delicacy and sensitivity that characterizes the drawings of the Florentine painter. The harsh cross-hatches and the heavy, bold line often distinguish the Florentine sculptor from the Florentine painter.

DOMENICO BECCAFUMI
(Siena ca. 1486-1551)

D4. *A Study for a Part of the Mosaic Frieze of the Siena Cathedral Pavement*, 1544

Pen and bistre wash; 8 x 11 5/8 inches
Lent by the Fogg Art Museum, Harvard University, Meta and Paul J. Sachs Bequest
Provenance: Giuseppe Vallardi (Lugt 1223); Blaisot (Lugt 263); Langton Douglas to Paul J. Sachs
Exhibitions: Century Club, New York, 1947; John Herron Museum of Art, Indianapolis, Ind., *Pontormo to Greco—The Age of Mannerism*, 1954, no. 7, repr.; The Detroit Institute of Arts, *Decorative Arts of the Italian Renaissance, 1400-1600*, Nov. 18, 1958-Jan. 4, 1959, 9A p. 25; The Baltimore Museum of Art, *Bacchiacca and His Friends*, 1961, no. 43.
Bibliography: Agnes Mongan and Paul Sachs, *Drawings in the Fogg Museum of Art*, Cambridge, Mass., 1946, no. 68, fig. 59; Robert O. Parks, *Pontormo to Greco—The Age of Mannerism*, 1954, no. 7, repr.

Although there have been opinions stating that this drawing is after the mosaic frieze of the Siena Cathedral Pavement, the drawing is generally accepted as a study for this project that Beccafumi worked on in 1544. There is a decisiveness and sureness of line that is not typical of an artist who is considered to have been more of a colorist than as a painter and draughtsman. His drawings for frescoes were generally more painterly, often done in tempera and emulsion. This drawing, however, was to be employed as a guide for a mosaicist rather than a painter . . . a discipline that required a more linear approach.

The Mosaic Frieze is not mentioned by Vasari, but Beccafumi's activities at the Siena Cathedral are. Although Beccafumi spent most of his life in and around Siena, he, as a youth (ca. 1510-12 and 1519) did go to Rome where he studied the works of Michelangelo, Raphael, and the antique statues and sarcophagi. This trip was to have a pronounced influence on Beccafumi's works. The

drawing is similar in many respects to Michelangelo's paintings as well as the sarcophagi. The tensions created by the muscular, foreshortened figures, struggling in a shallow space, are evident in both the works of Michelangelo and this drawing by Beccafumi. "While their action is spirited, it is also a little frantic and suggests their inner, spiritual tensions . . ." (Parks, *Pontormo to Greco*, no. 7).

DOMENICO BECCAFUMI
(Siena ca. 1486-1551)

D5. *The Descent from the Cross*

Pen, brown ink and wash with grey wash over black chalk; 14 1/2 x 11 inches
Lent by the Achenbach Foundation for Graphic Arts, California Palace of the Legion of Honor,
Provenance: Giorgio Vasari; Pierre Crozat; Gabriel Huquier, Paris; purchased 1932 with funds of the Senator James D. Phelan Bequest from O'Hara, Livermore and Arthur Baken, Inc., San Francisco.
Exhibitions: Mills College Art Gallery, Oakland, Cal., *Old Master Drawings*, Oct. 24-Dec. 12, 1937 and Portland Museum of Art, Portland, Ore., Dec. 16, 1937-Jan. 16, 1938, cat. no. 4, repr.; Pomona College Art Gallery, Claremont, Cal., *Mannerism*, 1963; The John and Mabel Ringling Museum of Art, Sarasota, Fla., *Master Drawings*, 1967; The University Art Museum, University of California, Berkeley, Cal., *Master Drawings from California Collections*, 1968, cat. 29:106, repr.
Bibliography: Pierre-Jean Mariette, "Description Sommaire des desseins des grandes maîtres . . . du cabinet de feu M. Crozat," Paris 1741, p. 7; A. Wyatt, "Il Libro dei Disegni del Vasari," *Gazette des Beaux-Arts*, 1859, IV, p. 350; Hans Tietze, "A Drawing by Beccafumi in San Francisco," *Pacific Art Review*, Summer 1942, p. 7, repr.

This handsome drawing plays several roles in this exhibition. On the lower right corner the inscription, "D. Builfumi micarino cauato **Del** libro di Vasari," identifies this sheet as once belonging to Vasari's celebrated collection. (See A. Wyatt, "Le Libro de Disegni del Vasari," *Gazette des Beaux Arts*, 1859, IV, 350). Vasari's impressive collection of drawings, assembled to supplement pictorially his *Le Vite de'Piu Eccellenti Pittori Scultori, e Architettori*, was bound in five volumes, and had examples representing artists from the Trecento to the third quarter of the sixteenth century. Unfortunately, this drawing no longer retains the decorative border (mount) that distinguished many of the drawings from Vasari's collection (for example see drawing by Federico Zuccaro, no. D25 in this exhibition).

No surviving painting has been connected with this drawing. Reflecting the influence of Raphael and particularly that of Michelangelo, Beccafumi's exploration of tonal values through the use of ink washes and black chalk is the most notable quality of the drawing.

Figures severely elongated create a composition of verticality, an economy of line, supplemented by broad areas of liberally applied wash creating figures of structure. Perhaps the most dramatic element in the drawing is the untreated white surface that gleams against the gradations of grey and black, producing a kind of luminous unreality.

The work is energetic, and the style is characteristic of Beccafumi's later works. It also presents the viewer with a startling contrast to the *Study for the Mosaic Pavement of Siena Cathedral,* no. D4 in the exhibition.

GIROLAMO MAZZOLA BEDOLI
(Parma 1500/5-1569)

D6. *Lucretia*

Watercolor heightened with gouache;
11 3/4 x 8 3/8 inches
Lent by Mr. & Mrs. Jacob M. Kaplan
Provenance: Nourri (sale, Paris 1785); Marquis C. de Valori (1820-1883), (Lugt 2500); Eugene Rodrigues, (Lugt 897); Henri Delacroix, collection mark in l.r; Jacques Seligman, New York, 1966.
Bibliography: Nourri Sale, Feb. 24-March 16, 1785, no. 433.

This drawing was first brought to the attention of Mr. A. E. Popham, after the scholar had published his catalogue raisonné on Bedoli's drawings (Popham, "The Drawings of Girolamo Bedoli," *Master Drawings,* II, No. 3, 1964, pp. 243-267, pls. 1-17). In a letter to Mrs. Kaplan, Popham attributed the drawing to Parmigianino's controversial cousin Bedoli, suggesting that the drawing may have been inspired by Parmigianino.

The drawing is unquestionably after Parmigianino. An engraving of *Lucretia* (Bartsch, XV, 17) by Enea Vico bears the inscription: "E.V./Fran. Par./Inventor", is very close to the Bedoli drawing (the engraving is reproduced in S. Freedberg, *Parmigianino, His Works in Painting,* Cambridge, 1950, p. 238 and ill. 119). The engraving is also similar to a double sided drawing *Studies for a Lucretia* in the Budapest Museum (reproduced in Freedberg, *ibid.,* ills. 118 a & b).

As the Bedoli drawing differs in some respects with both the Vico engraving and the Parmigianino drawing, it is difficult to conclude the exact source of Bedoli's composition. Vico's engraving is the most likely to be an accurate account of Parmigianino's painting, and Bedoli, though indebted to his cousin for many of his forms and style, may have wished to retain some degree of individuality. This would account for the differences in the directions in which Lucretia looks (in the engraving she looks toward the upper left and in the drawing to the upper right), as well as the change from a landscape seen through a window in the engraving to a paneled wall in the drawing.

In this drawing and the Vico engraving we may have a record of what Vasari calls Parmigianino's last and one of his best works (*Lives,* III, p. 12). Stylistically, the drawing relates more closely to Bedoli's *Eve in an Oval* (Louvre, no. 6503), a drawing that Popham dates ca. 1538-1540 (op. cit., pl. 4b, cat. no. 18). Parmigianino's death in 1540 is further evidence of the value of the engraving and the drawing as a record.

BENVENUTO CELLINI
(Florence 1500-1571)

D7. *Standing Nude Male Figure with a Club*

Pen and brown ink, brown wash; 16 1/8 x 7 3/4 inches
Lent by Mr. Ian Woodner
Provenance: John Barnard (Lugt 1419); Sir Thomas Lawrence (Lugt 2445).
Inscriptions: In pen and brown ink at lower right corner: *alla porta di fontana/Bellio. di bronzo p piu/ di dua volte il vivo . . ./erano dua variati* (at the portal of Fontainebleau, in bronze, twice life-size—there were two versions).
Exhibitions: The Newark Museum, Newark, New Jersey, *Old Master Drawings,* 1960, no. 25 repr.; The Metropolitan Museum of Art, *Drawings from New York Collections I—The Italian Renaissance,* Nov. 8, 1965-Jan 9, 1966, no. 82, repr.
Bibliography: Jacob Bean and Felice Stampfle, *Drawings from New York Collections—I—The Italian Renaissance,* Greenwich, New York Graphic Society, 1965, no. 82. repr.

Stampfle and Bean consider this drawing to date from Cellini's period in Fontainebleau, and corresponding to Cellini's description of the sculptured portal for the Chateau de Fontainebleau. "Instead of columns . . . I fashioned two satyrs, one upon each side. The first of these was in somewhat more than half-relief, lifting one hand to support the cornice and holding a thick club in the other; his face was fiery and menacing, instilling fear into the beholders . . . Though I call them satyrs, they showed nothing of the satyr except little horns and a goatish head; all the rest of the form was human." (Bean and Stampfle, no. 104 and *Autobiography,* tr. J. A. Symonds, New York, p. 272)

Unfortunately the portal was never completed. Only the bronze lunette with the nymph of Fontainebleau, in the Louvre, is known. Stampfle and Bean relate this drawing to a black chalk study of Juno, also in the Louvre (op. cit., no. 104).

ROSSO FIORENTINO
(Florence 1495-Fontainebleau 1540)

D8. *Standing Youth*

Red chalk on white paper; 7 9/16 x 3 3/8 inches
Lent by Mr. Janos Scholz

Exhibitions: Mills College, Oakland, 1961; Neumeyer-Scholz, 1961; "Italian Drawings," University of Wisconsin, 1964, no. 34, plate 16.
Bibliography: Charles de Tolnay, *Michelangelo,* 1943-1960, Vol. III, fig. 272.
Giovanni Battista di Jacopo, called "Il Rosso," probably received his early training from Andrea del Sarto, Fra Bartolomeo, and the graphics of Albrecht Duerer. Like so many of the Florentines, he could not escape the influence of Michelangelo. The *Sistine Ceiling,* the cartoon for the *Battle of Cascina* and Michelangelo's sculpture made a lasting impression on Rosso. This study, attributed to Rosso, is after Michelangelo's *David* (ca. 1530, Museo Nazionale del Bargello, Forence).
Employing red chalk, Rosso found in Michelangelo's sculptures, the turning, dynamic forms that were to characterize his panels. Rosso often placed individual forms in narrow and shallow spacial niches. The drawing compares to the numerous allegorical drawings that he had engraved by Gian Giacomo Caraglio.

PROSPERO FONTANA
(Bologna 1512-1597)

D9. *Study for a Ceiling Decoration*

Pen and wash over red and black chalk; 14 3/8 x 9 5/16 inches
Lent by the Art Institute of Chicago, the Leonora Hall Gurley Memorial Collection
Inscriptions: upper left corner, *Fontana Prospero*
Provenance: J. J. Lindeman (Lugt 1479A)
Exhibitions: Art Institute of Chicago, 1922
In 1922 Ulrich Middledorf attributed this drawing to Fontana, calling it a study for a ceiling by Prospero in the Palazzo Parilla in Bologna.
More recently, Philip Pouncey, John Shearman and Edmund Pillsbury have suggested that the study is by Vasari. It is thought to be an early study for the Sala of Clement VII in the Palazzo Vecchio. In support of this position, Dr. Wiener has pointed out that the device, called *Cander Illaesus,* above the picture of the bearded old man (botton, center) was that of Pope Clement VII (Tervaient, "Symbols dans l'Art," *Soleil,* 1958, p. 358)

PROSPERO FONTANA
(Bologna 1512-1597)

D10. *Thetis Ordering from Vulcan the Armour of Achilles*

Pen and bistre, bistre wash on blue paper; 9 5/16 x 4 5/8 inches
Lent by Mr. Janos Scholz
Exhibitions: The John Herron Museum of Art, Indianapolis, Ind., *Pontormo to Greco—The Age of Mannerism,* 1964, no. 34, repr.
This drawing, traditionally attributed to Prospero Fontana, depicts Thetis, mother of Achilles, before Vulcan, the god of fire in the act of forging and smelting. Apparently she is ordering armour for Achilles to enable her son to shed the elements of mortality that he had inherited from his father. However, we should also note the several urns and vases that surround Vulcan. As part of her program to make Achilles immortal, Thetis anointed her son with ambrosia during the day and held him in the fire in the evening.
Fontana was influenced by Parmigianino, Michelangelo, the followers of Raphael, and Vasari. The figure of Thetis also indicates the influence of Perino del Vaga if compared with Perino's drawing of the *Guerriero* (Louvre, no. 624) and no. D24 in this exhibition. Fontana had worked with Perino in Genoa and certainly knew the older master's works. Nor should we underestimate the influence of Vasari. This drawing was influenced by Vasari's mature style of the 1560's, as can be seen in the fluidity of the lines.

GIOVANNI BATTISTA NALDINI
(Florence 1537-Florence 1591)

D11. *Study for the Virgin, St. Agnes, St. Helena, and Other Saints,* ca. 1571-1576

Pen, brown ink and brown wash on paper prepared with red wash, perhaps faded; 7 1/2 x 7 1/8 inches
Lent by Mr. Edmund Pillsbury
Provenance: *Padre Resta* (inscribed in pen and brown ink at the lower center, *m 157,* and annotated on the mount with Resta's original attribution to Cesare Nebbia); H. S. Olivier (Lugt 1373); sold at Christie's, 27 June 1967 (lot 175) to Pillsbury.
Bibliography: Peter Cannon Brookes, "Three Notes on Maso da San Friano," *Burlington Magazine,* CVII, April 1965, pp. 192-197 (see ill. 31 for 'modello')
Originally attributed to Cesare Nebbia, this wash drawing is a study for a *modello,* "The Ascension above the Virgin, St. Agnes, St. Helena, and Other Saints" now located in the Ashmolean Museum in Oxford. The altar-piece for which the drawing and *modello* were executed, is now lost, apparently destroyed in a fire in S. Maria del Carmine in 1771 (Peter Cannon Brookes, "Three Notes on Maso da San Friano," *Burlington Magazine,* April 1965, pp. 192-197). The altar-piece was originally scheduled to be painted by Maso da San Friano (see Brookes, ill. 32) and Naldini's *modello* corresponds in some detail to Maso's preparatory study (Uffizi, 602s). However, Maso died in 1571 and between this time and the death of Elena Ottonelli in 1576 (donor for the altar-piece), the commission was transferred to Naldini.
Although Naldini retains the relative position of several of the figures from Maso's drawing, he introduces several variations which reflect his indebtedness to Vasari. Most noteworthy is his treatment of the Virgin. It is very similar in attitude to Vasari's "Allegory of the Immaculate Conception" for Santi Apostoli (see Barocchi,

Vasari Pittore, colorplate, XI, also ill. 18, and *Mostra di Disegni del Vasari e Della Sua Cerchia,* plates 4, 5, and 8). Other Vasari followers were to borrow from the master. Prospero Fontana's treatment of the Virgin is undoubtedly inspired by Vasari (Uffizi no. 1078 S, repr. *Vasari e della Sua Cerchia,* pl. 32) and is very close to Naldini's rendering of the Blessed Mother. The figure on the far left of Naldini's drawing appears to be a variation on the central figure from Vasari's *Tree of Love* (Louvre, no. 2169) which in turn Vasari seems to have borrowed from Michelangelo's *Battle of Cascina.*

Florentine drawings vary in form and purpose. Some are conceived in terms of the line only. In this instance, form is the main preoccupation and the artist shows little concern for line. He is more concerned with light and its effect on form. It is likely that there were other drawings by Naldini for the *modello* that dealt with the line.

GIOVANNI BATTISTA NALDINI
(Florence, 1537-1590)

D12. *Project for a Ceiling,* (Study for the *Oratory of Antonio Giacomini,* Sala Grande, Palazzo Vecchio, Florence), ca. 1563-1566

Pen and brush, brown ink on white paper; 3 7/8 x 8 5/8 inches
Lent by Mr. Janos Scholz
Inscriptions: "sogliano" l.l. of central sheet
Exhibitions: Mills College Art Gallery, Oakland, Calif., *Drawings from Tuscany and Umbria, 1350-1700,* 1961; Department of Art History Gallery, University of Wisconsin, Milwaukee, *Italian Drawings,* 1964, No. 39, ill. 19 (as Giorgio Vasari).
Bibliography: Neumeyer-Scholz, Drawings from Tuscany and Umbria 1350-1700 Oakland, 1961; Jack Wasserman, *Italian Drawings,* Milwaukee, 1964, No. 39, ill. 19; Gunther Thiem, "Neuentdeckte Zeichnungen Vasaris und Naldinis fur die Sala Grande des Palazzo Vecchio in Florenz," *Zeitschrift fur Kunstgeschichte,* 1968, pages 143-150, fig. i.
This drawing was attributed to Giorgio Vasari until 1968 when Gunther Thiem reattributed it to Battista Naldini, one of Vasari's principle assistants at the Palazzo Vecchio. As the sheet compares favorably to other drawings by Vasari for the ceiling of the Sala Grande, the present attribution is open to discussion.
In his monumental essays, Thiem reconstructs the second plan of the ceiling of the Sala Grande. The plan, outlining the themes of the thirty-nine panels composing the ceiling is in the Uffizi (no. 7979A) and reproduced in Thiem, "Vasari's Entwürfe für die Gemalde in der Sala Grande des Palazzo Vecchio zu Florenz," *Zeitschrift für Kunstgeschichte,* 1960, II, fig. 1). Thiem states that these drawings correspond to panels 24, 27 and 30 (numbers 1 through 39 were assigned to the panels). "It contains the sketched suggestions for panels 24 (*Piano di Val di Cascini*), 27

(*Princjipio della Guerra di Pisa et consiglio di cittadjni a farla* which is also known as *Arringa di Antonio Giacomini* on the basis of *Ragionamenti*), and 30 (*Livorno Mare*) (translated from Thiem, "Neuentdeckte Zeichnungen Vasaris und Naldinis für die Sala Grande des Palazzo Vecchio in Florenz," *Zeitschrift für Kunstgeschichte,* 1968, p. 145). These three sketches, joined with the two sheets attached from the Fogg Art Museum (no. D42), play a major role in Thiem's reconstruction.

LELIO ORSI
(Reggio 1511-Novellara 1587)

D13. *Study for the 'Walk to Emmaus,'* London National Gallery

Crayon, heightened with white on brown paper; 13 5/8 x 10 1/8 inches
Lent by the Wadsworth Atheneum. The Ella Gallup Sumner and Mary Catlin Sumner Collection
Provenance: Purchased from Durlacher Bros., London, England in 1937
Exhibitions: Wadsworth Atheneum, Hartford, Conn., *Life of Christ,* 1948, no. 158; Detroit Institute of Arts, *Sixty Drawings from the Wadsworth Atheneum,* Hartford, 1948; Wadsworth Atheneum, *In Retrospect—Twenty-One Years of Museum Collecting,* 1949, no. 50; The John Herron Museum of Art, Indianapolis, Ind., *Pontormo to Greco—The Age of Mannerism,* 1954, no. 31, repr.; The School of Fine Arts, The University of Connecticut, Storrs, Conn., *The Figure in Mannerist and Baroque Drawings,* 1967.
Bibliography: Florence Kossoff, "Lelio Orsi and the Walk to Emmaus," *Master Drawings,* 1966, IV, no. 4, pp. 415-418, plate 30.
Florence Kossoff cites four drawings (Louvre, Inv. No. 6686; Collection of Mr. Charles M. Muskavitch, Sacramento, California; Geneo, Palazzo Rosso, Inv. No. 572 and Wadsworth Atheneum) that are in some way connected with Orsi's panel, *The Walk to Emmaus,* in the London National Gallery (no. D13a). She convincingly demonstrates the Wadsworth Atheneum drawing to be a copy after the panel, yet by the hand of Orsi. (Kossoff, "Lelio Orsi and the Walk to Emmaus," *Master Drawings,* 1966, IV, pp. 415-418).
The four drawings present a unique group as they represent three practices common in the sixteenth century. The Louvre version is the preliminary study for the panel, whereas both the Wadsworth Atheneum and Muskavitch drawings are copies after the panel. The Wadsworth Atheneum drawing was the first of the two copies as it is less mechanical in execution. Orsi probably had other requests for the subject that led him to make these copies. The fourth drawing, representing another practice, is a poor copy, by a student rather than Orsi.
This is not the only instance where Orsi made copies after his own compositions. The Princeton

Art Museum, the Chatsworth Collection and the Galeria Estense, Modena, all possess drawings titled "Project for a Decoration of a Facade" that are similar and by Orsi.

LELIO ORSI
(Reggio 1511-Novellara 1587)

D14. *Design for a Facade Decoration*

Pen and brown ink; 8 5/16 x 11 1/16 inches (two sheets joined horizontally at the center).
Lent by Mr. Janos Scholz
Inscriptions: signed, inscribed in pen and brown ink at lower left margin *lolio*.
Provenance: H. Beckmann (Lugt S. 2756a)
Exhibitions: Hamburg, Scholz Exhibition, 1963, no. 103, plate 21; the Metropolitan Museum of Art, New York, *Drawings from New York Collections—I—The Italian Renaissance,* Nov. 8, 1965-Jan 9, 1966, no. 106, repr.
Bibliography: Jacob Bean and Felice Stampfle, *Drawings from New York Collections—I—The Italian Renaissance,* Greenwich, New York Graphic Society 1965, no. 106, repr.
Lelio Orsi was essentially a provincial artist who came under the influence of Michelangelo (through a trip to Rome), and Correggio and Parmigianino (probably because of the proximity of Novellara with Parma). The influence of the later artist is perhaps most noticeable in this drawing,—particularly when looking at the female figures in this composition.
Orsi's drawings far outnumber his paintings. This is largely due to his practice of making several drawings of the same subject (see discussion of no. D17). Orsi also painted several exterior frescoes that no longer survive. Bean and Stampfle suggest that this drawing may have been for a palace facade that has since been destroyed (Bean, Stampfle, *Drawings from New York Collections,* 1965, no. 106).
It is difficult to determine the iconography of this drawing. On the upper tier, to the right, a dancing female is enclosed by an arcade, caryatids, and putti. To the left of her is a rocky landscape sheltering an embracing couple whose activities have attracted three wind gods. The bottom tier depicts a second female framed by an arcade and surrounded by caryatids and putti.
Florence Kossoff calls our attention to a similar scheme of caryatids in the fragments of interior frescoes removed from the Casino di Sopra in Novellara (Kossoff, *Mostra di Lelio Orsi,* Reggio Emilia, 1950, nos. 18-35) and Stampfle and Bean point out a pen study for similar caryatids in the Seattle Art Museum (op. cit., no. 106).

FRANCESCO MAZZOLA, called
PARMIGIANINO
(Parma 1503-Casal Maggiore 1540)

D15. *Three Studies of Putti and of a Seated Boy (recto); Studies in Red Chalk of a*

Woman's Head of a Putto, and of a Fence (verso)

Red chalk; 7 3/16 x 5 13/16 inches (red chalk on white paper)
Lent by Mr. Janos Scholz
Exhibitions: Indiana University, Bloomington, Ind., *Drawings of the Italian Renaissance from the Scholz Collection,* 1958, No. 35, repr.; Hamburg, Scholz Exhibition, 1963, No. 108, pl. 22; Yale University, New Haven, Conn., *Italian Drawings from the Collection of Janos Scholz,* 1964, No. 43, repr. No. 10; The Metropolitan Museum of Art, New York, *Drawings from New York Collection—I—The Italian Renaissance,* Nov. 8, 1965-Jan. 9, 1966, No. 89, repr.
Bibliography: Jacob Bean and Felice Stampfle, *Drawings from New York Collections—I—The Italian Renaissance,* Greenwich, New York Graphic Society, 1965, no. 89, repr.
Although this handsome sheet has not been related to any painting, it is an unusually fine study, characteristic of Parmigianino's hand. A. E. Popham dates the drawing early in the artist's career, probably in the early 1520's before Parmigianino went to Rome (Bean-Stampfle, *Drawings from New York Collections,* 1965, no. 89).
Vasari's introductory remarks about Parmigianino epitomize the qualities found in this drawing. The sensitivity and grace are common qualities in Parmigianino's chalk drawings. Vasari credits Parmigianino for his "vivacity of invention" (*Lives,* III, p. 6). The manner in which he treats the youthful figures, boldly foreshortened, with a resolute strength and yet with a softness, is unlike Parmigianino's contemporaries. Structure of form is created through the treatment of surface rather than through inner structural elements. The result of Parmigianino's approach to the human figure is an elegance and refinement admired and praised by Vasari.

FRANCESCO MAZZOLA, called
PARMIGIANINO
(Parma 1503-Casal Maggiore 1540)

D16. *Study for Lucretia,* ca. 1524-1527

Red chalk heightened with white; 7 5/16 x 5 1/8 inches
Lent by Mr. Janos Scholz
Provenance: Crozat; Banks; Triquetti; Goldstein
Exhibitions: *Pontormo to Greco—The Age of Mannerism,* John Herron Museum of Art, Indianapolis, 1954, No. 22, repr.
Bibliography: Robert O. Parks, *Pontormo to Greco—The Age of Mannerism,* 1954, No. 22, repr.
According to Sydney Freedberg, this study was made during Parmigianino's trip to Rome in 1524-1527 (Parks, *Pontormo to Greco,* no. 22). Parmigianino was to treat the subject on several occasions. This drawing was perhaps one of the earliest and most unconventional. Vasari records in the "Life" of Parmigianino a much later paint-

ing of Lucretia but eliminates any possible connection with this drawing when he states that it was Parmigianino's last painting before his death ("Lives," III, p. 12).

This drawing is symptomatic of the anti-classical style that Friedlaender described (*Mannerism and Anti-Mannerism in Italian Painting*). By comparison to the other Parmigianino drawing in this exhibition (no. D15), the artist demonstrates an increasing interest in surface movements, gestures, rhythms, etc. The stress is placed on the massive heavy limbs of Lucretia as she shifts her weight, impaling herself on the sword. Parmigianino creates a tension that we are compelled to share with Lucretia.

JACOPO DA CARRUCCI, called PONTORMO
(Pontormo 1494-Florence 1557)

D17. *Bust of a Nude Youth* (Study for the Virgin, *Deposition,* Altar-piece, S. Felicita) ca. 1526-1527.

Red chalk; 6 3/16 x 5 inches
Lent by Mr. Janos Scholz
Provenance: Piancastelli, Brandegee.
Exhibitions: The John Herron Museum of Art, Indianapolis, Ind., *Pontormo to Greco-The Age of Mannerism,* 1954, no. 10, repr.; Indiana University, Bloomington, Ind., *Drawings of the Italian Renaissance from the Scholz Collection,* 1958, no. 38, repr.; Mills College Art Gallery, Oakland, Cal., *Drawings from Tuscany and Umbria,* 1961, no. 70; also Scholz exhibitions: 1963 Hamburg; 1964 Koln; Department of Art History Gallery, University of Wisconsin, Milwaukee, *Italian Drawings,* 1964; 1968 London, Liverpool, Edinburgh, British Arts Council, 1965, no. 74.
Bibliography: Robert O. Parks, *Pontormo to Greco—The Age of Mannerism,* 1954, no. 10; Bernard Berenson, *I Disegni dei Pittori Fiorentini,* Milan, 1961, 3 vols. no. 2256; Janet Cox Rearick, *The Drawings of Pontormo,* Cambridge, 1964, vol. 1 of 2 vols., p. 399, no. A234 (as a 16th century copy).
This study for Pontormo's altarpiece of the *Deposition* in S. Felicita, was considered a 16th century copy after a drawing in the Uffizi (no. 6666F) by Janet Cox Rearick (*The Drawings of Pontormo,* 1964, p. 399, no. A234). Miss Rearick discredits the Scholz study on the grounds that there is no other example in Pontormo's work of this kind of repetition.
The drawing, however, has been accepted as Pontormo by A. E. Popham, Philip Pouncey, Charles de Tolnay, Agnes Mongan, J. Byam Shaw, John Gere and Lugt. Dr. Ivan Fenyo has expressed orally that the drawing is not by the hand of a copyist. He feels that it pre-dates the drawing in the Uffizi. The Scholz drawing is less elaborate that the Uffizi study, while the modeling of the torso, the neck and the attachment of the head are more convincingly rendered in the drawing exhibited.

The Florentine draughtsman often made several studies for paintings. This may be the instance where Pontormo decided to work out, in greater detail, a second study for the S. Felicita *Deposition.*

FRANCESCO MORANDINI, called IL POPPI
(Poppi, Casentino 1544-Florence 1597)

D18. *Manna in the Wilderness*

Red and black chalk on white paper; 10 1/16 x 7 7/8 inches
Lent by Mr. Janos Scholz
Provenance: Cav. Giovanni Piancastelli, Rome; Mrs. Edward D. Brandegee, Boston
Exhibitions: The John Herron Museum of Art, Indianapolis, Ind., *Pontormo to Greco—The Age of Mannerism,* 1954, No. 14, repr. (as Rosso Fiorentino); Indiana University, Bloomington, Ind., *Drawings of the Italian Renaissance from the Scholz Collection,* 1958; Mills College Art Gallery, Oakland, Calf., *Drawings from Tuscany and Umbria,* 1961; Department of Art History Gallery, University of Wisconsin, Milwaukee, *Italian Drawings,* 1964, No. 33, ill. 15 (as Rosso Fiorentino).
Bibliography: Robert O. Parks, *Pontormo to Greco—The Age of Mannerism,* 1954, No. 14, repr. (as Rosso Fiorentino); G. Gilbert, *Drawings of the Italian Renaissance from the Scholz Collection,* 1958; Neumeyer-Scholz, *Drawings from Tuscany and Umbria 1350-1700,* 1961; Jack Wasserman, *Italian Drawings,* 1964, No. 33, ill. 15 (as Rosso Fiorentino).
Formerly attributed to Rosso Fiorentino, this drawing is now assigned to Poppi. Although it has not been possible to discover the purpose of the drawing, the style is characteristically that of Poppi. The figures are constructed with undulating short, crisp strokes of chalk, and strengthened by parallel lines of chalk. Poppi considers form first in terms of the outline and then analyzes it in terms of geometric units. He plays with space, thrusting limbs toward the viewer from the shallow space that encloses the figures. Movements are strengthened by darker lines, faces are reduced to basic areas seen as shadows.
This drawing can be compared to Uffizi no. 471 F, "Ulysses and the Winds" (reproduced in Barocchi, *Mostra di Disegni del Vasari e della Sua Cerchia,* pl. 56) as well as the *Falling of the Manna* in the Boscomarengo, Santa Croce (reproduced in Barocchi, *Vasari Pittore,* pl. V).

FRANCESCO DEI ROSSI, called FRANCESCO SALVIATI
(Florence 1510-Rome 1563)

D19. *Design for a Fantastic Emblem*

Pen and brown ink, brown wash; 7 1/2 x 7 3/8 inches
Lent by Mr. Janos Scholz
Provenance: Richard Cosway (Lugt 628)

Inscriptions: In pen and ink at the l.r. "Julio Romano"

Exhibitions: Mills College Art Gallery, Oakland, Calf., *Drawings from Tuscany and Umbria 1350-1700*, 1961, No. 74; Hamburg, Scholz Exhibition, 1963, no. 141, plate 33; The Metropolitan Museum of Art, New York, *Drawings from New York Collections—I—The Italian Renaissance,* Nov. 8, 1965-Jan. 9, 1966, No. 103, repr.

Bibliography: Jacob Bean and Felice Stampfle, *Drawings from New York Collections—I—The Italian Renaissance,* Greenwich New York Graphic Society, 1965, No. 103, repr.

Fantastic animals of such invention were common creations by the sixteenth century Roman and Florentine artists. Animal grotesqueries appeared often from the hands of Giulio Romano, Perino del Vaga, and Francesco Salviati. The designs often served as preliminary sketches for the decoration of door knobs, lamps, candlesticks, vases, ceilings, etc. Giulio Romano is perhaps best known for this kind of invention, which is probably the reason for the inscription that the drawing bears.

However, the style is not that of Giulio Romano, rather it is that of Vasari's close friend Francesco Salviati. In this drawing, Salviati has created a horse with two heads, perched on a small base. One of the horse's heads strains upward, breathing fire, and attracting a huge moth or butterfly. The Louvre owns another drawing (Inv. 12,085) which is a variant on this design and is listed as Anonymous Italian. In the Louvre drawing the horse is replaced by an elephant with a human head (Bean, Stampfle, *Drawings from New York Collections,* no. 103). Pouncey has also called our attention to a similar drawing in the British Museum as well as a pen version of the same animal in the collection of Mr. Hans Schaeffer, New York, which is attributed to Perino del Vaga. The inscription on the banderole is illegible and does not assist us with determining the purpose of the drawing.

FRANCESCO DEI ROSSI, called FRANCESCO SALVIATI
(Florence 1510-Rome 1563)

D20. *Warrior Kneeling before an Enthroned Pope* (Study for the Walls of the Salotto in the Palazzo Farnese in Rome)

Pen and brown ink, brown wash, heightened with white, over traces of black chalk, horizontal pen-line at center; several layers of *pentimenti* pasted on the foreground; 8 1/4 x 10 7/16 inches

Lent by The Cooper-Hewitt Museum of Decorative Arts and Design, Smithsonian Institution

Provenance: Giovanni Piancastelli, Rome; Eleanor and Sarah Hewitt

Exhibitions: The Cooper-Union Museum, New York, American Federation of Arts, *Five Centuries of drawings, The Cooper-Union Centennial Exhibition,* 1959-1961, No. 4; The Metropolitan Museum of Art, New York, *Drawings from New York Collections—I—The Italian Renaissance,* Nov. 8, 1965-Jan. 9, 1966, No. 101, repr.

Bibliography: Richard P. Wunder, *Five Centuries of Drawings. The Cooper Union Centennial Exhibition,* 1959-1961, No. 4; Jacob Bean and Felice Stampfle, *Drawings from New York Collections—I—The Italian Renaissance,* Greenwich, New York Graphic Society, 1965, No. 101, repr.

In 1961 Richard Wunder suggested that this drawing was a study for the fresco in the Palazzo Farnese, Rome, depicting Pope Eugenius commissioning Rannuccio Farnese as the military defender of the Papal States (no. D20a). Both the drawing and the fresco show Pope Eugenius IV giving the baton of papal commandment to Farnese.

Even though there have been substantial changes made from the drawing to the fresco, it is safe to conclude that this drawing does represent the very early stages of Salviati's plans for the fresco. The most significant part of the composition has remained relatively unaltered from the drawing to the fresco, while the crowd that witnesses the scene is noticeably altered. These changes are perhaps due to two factors. The first being Salviati's own indecision which is clearly evident in the changes that are already made on the initial drawing. The *pentimenti* added in the foreground indicates that Salviati was already deviating from his original design. The *river god* image added in the right foreground was clearly inspired by the *river god* in Marcantonio Raimondi's engraving after Raphael's drawing of *The Judgment of Paris.* The second reason for change could be due to the fact that Taddeo Zuccaro completed the fresco in 1553, after Salviati's designs.

This drawing relates to another group of drawings by Salviati at Windsor, also representing the history of the papacy (Popham, Wilde, *Italian Drawings at Windsor,* nos. 888-890).

The Florentine artist often deviated from his initial design. This drawing is a very quick, almost hasty sketch. The figures are suggested with an economy of line and wash. Salviati appears more concerned with the over-all design rather than with individual elements.

JAN VAN DER STRAET, called STRADANUS
(Bruges 1523-Florence 1605)

D21. *Nobilitas*

Pen and brush, brown ink over black crayon on white paper: 4 1/4 x 5 13/16 inches

Lent by Mr. Janos Scholz

Provenance: Piancastelli; Brandegee; R. Wien

Bibliography: Michel N. Benisovich; "The Drawings of Stradanus (Jan van der Straet) in the Cooper-Union for the Arts of Decoration, New York," *The Art Bulletin,* pp. 249-254.

D22. *The Annunciation*

Pen and brush, brown ink, blue wash on white
paper; 4 3/16 x 2 7/8 inches
Lent by Mr. Janos Scholz.
Provenance: Piancastelli; Brandegee.
Exhibitions: Art Gallery, University of Notre
Dame, *The Life of Christ,* 1964, no. 64; same,
The Life of the Virgin Mary, 1967, no. 46.

D23. *Christ Washing the Feet of His Disciples*

Pen and brush, brown ink and red watercolor
over black crayon on white paper; 5 3/16 x 4 1/16
inches
Provenance: Piancastelli; Brandegee.
Exhibitions: Art Gallery, University of Notre
Dame, *The Life of Christ,* 1964, no. 65.
Lent by Mr. Janos Scholz
These drawings, formerly in the collection of
Mr. Giovanni Piancastelli, Director of the Bor-
ghese Gallery, are but three of the over three
hundred drawings by Jan van der Straet in New
York collections (The Cooper Union Museum for
the Arts of Decoration, New York, has 312 in
its collection).
The Flemish born Stradanus was one of the principle assistants to Vasari at the Palazzo Vecchio.
These sketches were probably done after the
biographer's death in 1574. They still, however,
retain the style developed by Vasari and his circle.
The initial drawing was outlined in crayon and
traced and elaborated with ink and wash. The
tracing was done in "a cursive script by a pen
which tears and burns the paper." (Bensovich,
The Drawings . . . , p. 250).
They cannot be considered finished drawings
since they were intended to be further elaborated
and turned over to engravers in Munich or Ant-
werp. Bensovich has reproduced examples where
the drawings were engraved, (*The Drawings . . .*
ills. la and lc, 2a and 2b-f).
It is difficult to date these drawings with accuracy.
Bensovich suggests that they could have been
done as early as 1575 but also raises the possibility that they could have "been lying dormant
in his portfolios." (*ibid.,* p. 250).
The drawings from the Scholz collection are of
interest to us for a variety of reasons: *The
Annunciation* because of its relationship to
Vasari's early works, notably the Notre Dame
panel (no. P17) and the Pierpont Morgan Library modello (no. D48); *Christ Washing the Feet
of His Disiples* because of its spacial arrangement and *Nobilitas* because of its allegorical
content.
Stradanus' sketchbook offered a wide variety of
subject matter, from hunting scenes (a series was
engraved by J. Collaert and dedicated to Cosimo
de' Medici), allegorical and Biblical themes, in-
dustrial and professional scenes, to those decorative in nature. The complete group offers a
penetrating insight of Western Europe in the
second half of the 16th century.

PERINO DEL VAGA
(Florence 1501-Rome 1547)

D24. *Scene From the History of Alexander the
Great*

Pen, brown ink and grey wash,
12 3/8 x 8 1/4 inches
Lent by Mr. Ian Woodner
Inscription: In old hand, lower left
Perino del Vaga
Exhibitions: *Master Drawings,* Jacques Seligman
and Company, Nov.-Dec. 1966.
Bibliography: Jacob Bean (review of *National Gal-
lery of Scotland: Catalogue of Italian Drawings*)
Master Drawings, vol. 71 No. 1, p. 57, pl. 38.
Perino del Vaga is considered one of the most im-
portant Florentines who paved the way for the
"second generation Mannerists." In 1515 he worked
with Giulio Romano in the *atelier* of Raphael.
Perino soon became Raphael's most gifted pupil for
fresco decoration. In 1523 he fled from Rome to
Florence where his impression on the youthful
Florentines, Vasari, Salviati, etc. was to be estab-
lished with the exposure of his cartoon for the
Campagnia dei Martire of *The Martyrdom of the
Ten Thousand under King Sapor in Persia* (see
D24a)
In 1528 Perino worked for the Doria family in
Genoa and in 1534 and 1536 he worked in the
Cathedral of Pisa. In 1539, Perino returned to
Rome where he undertook the decoration of Castel
Sant 'Angelo.
Perino's influence on Vasari is readily apparent in
No. D31. Perino's style is characterized by an
assimilation of Raphael's classicism with Michel-
angelo's formalism. Perino's contact with Rosso
Fiorentino and Parmigianino in Rome contributed
to the development of Perino's elegant and decorative style.
The drawing exhibited here is a study for the fresco
in the Sala Paolina in the Castel Sant 'Angelo. The
vibrant drawing, dramatically lit from the upper
left, depicts a group of figures surrounding two
sarcophagi. To the left in profile, is the figure of
Alexander the Great. In the background, the mass
of figures are tightly compressed into a shallow
space. The decorative elements of the sarcophagi
reflect Romano's influence on Perino del Vaga's
Scene From the History of Alexander the Great.
According to Mr. Ian Woodner, Philip Pouncey
has confirmed that the drawing is a study by Perino
for one of the five colossal monochrome frescoes of
the story of Alexander in the Sala Paolino. The
only other study known for this project is in the
collection of Mr. and Mrs. John Gere. Both drawings show some variation from the frescoes.
Perino was working on this project at his death in
1547.

TADDEO ZUCCARO
(Sant 'Angelo in Vado 1529-Rome 1566)

D25. *The Sermon of St. John the Baptist* (verso)
Kneeling Man (recto)

Pen and brush, brown ink, heightened with white on blue paper (verso): black and white chalk on blue paper; (the border is in pen and brush, golden-brown ink); 16 9/16 x 11 1/16 inches
Provenance: Giorgio Vasari; Bentick; Walpole.
Lent by Mr. Janos Scholz
Inscriptions: On mount by Vasari; "TADDEO ZVCHERO/DA S. AGNOLO/PITTORE" (verso) "TADDEO ZVCHERO DA S. AGNOLO PIT." (recto).
Exhibitions: The John Herron Museum of Art, Indianapolis, Ind., *Pontormo to Greco—The Age of Mannerism*, 1954, no. 42, repr.; Hamburg, Scholz Exhibition, 1963; Koln, Scholz Exhibition, 1964; The Metropolitan Museum of Art, 1965 (no catalogue).
This double-sided drawing was once in Vasari's celebrated collection. Unfortunately, the Vasari mount has been trimmed. The subject of each side of the drawing is open to question. Robert Parks listed the subject of the recto, "Kneeling Man," as possibly being a study for a "Christ in the Garden of Gethsemene." (*Pontormo to Greco*, 1954, no. 42). Both the titles, "Christ in Limbo" and "The Sermon of St. John the Baptist" have been suggested for the verso. The latter seems more probable, despite the lack of certain iconographic requirements, i.e. no evidence of the "Ecce Agnus Dei" on the banner.
The drawing is a fine example of the exciting effects Taddeo produced in his chalk and pen drawings. One can sense the absolute ease and freedom of Taddeo's stroke.

JACOPO ZUCCHI (attributed to)
(Florence 1541-1589/1590)

D26. *Design for a Catafalque of Cosimo the Great,* 1574

Pen and brown ink with brown wash over black chalk; 15 1/16 x 10 3/8 inches
Lent by The Pierpont Morgan Library
Provenance: P. & D. Colnaghi and Co., Ltd.
Bibliography: Felice Stampfle, "Fourteenth Report to the Fellows of the Pierpont Morgan Library," New York, 1965/1966, pp. 106-107 (listed as anonymous)
Inscriptions: Upper center, *Insom Zuccari;* in *cartouche, MAG COSMUS / ETRURIE*
Plan I inscribed: *Pisa/carara/fiorenza/siena*
Plan II inscribed: *cavaliere* (or *cavalieri*)/ *creatione/trionfo/coronatione*
Plan III inscribed: *liberalita/carita/fortitudinel/ justizia*

D27. *Drawing of a Catafalque,* 1574

Pen and brown ink, and brown wash, over a preliminary drawing in black chalk, with the aid of a straightedge; 15 3/4 x 10 3/4 inches
Lent by Mr. Edmund Pillsbury
Provenance: From an album of Tuscan and Perugian drawings put together by an Italian collector at the end of the 19th century; P. & D. Colnaghi and Co., Ltd. (sold 1965); Herbert Bier, London (sold 1967).

Exhibitions: P. & D. Colnaghi and Co., Ltd., London, Exhibition of 17th and 18th century Italian Sculpture, Feb. 19-March 12, 1965, No. 25, pl. XV.
Bibliography: E. Borsook, "The Funeral of Cosimo I," *Mitteilungen des Kunsthistorisches Institutes in Florenz,* 1965-1966, XII, p. 53, fig. 10; Edmund Pillsbury, "An Unknown Project for the Palazzo Vecchio Courtyard," *Mitteilungen des Kunsthistorisches Institutes in Florenz,* 1969, XIV, p. 64, note 22.
On April 21st, 1574, Grand Duke Cosimo the Great died. In honor of his death, catafalques were erected throughout Italy. The two drawings exhibited here from the collections of Mr. Edmund Pillsbury and The Pierpont Morgan Library are studies for one of those catafalques.
The drawings were initially listed as "school of Vasari" and later attributed to Francesco Morandini (called Poppi) by Borsok. Philip Pouncey is responsible for the attribution of the Pillsbury drawing to Zucchi. The Morgan Library drawing, by the same hand, should also bear the same attribution.
At the time of Cosimo's death, Zucchi was in Rome. Pillsbury, on the basis of documents, has verbally suggested that the drawings may have been for the catafalque built in S. Giovanni del Fiorentini or some other church in Rome. The drawings were probably used for the presentation of Zucchi's ideas. The projects may or may not have been executed according to these designs.
Of the two, the Morgan Library drawing is far more complete. Zucchi has included on this sheet a complicated decorative scheme. Three cross-section drawings (right side of the drawing) indicate the sculpted virtues to be included and a sketch on the upper right corner shows the back side of the catafalque.
The Pillsbury drawing is less complex, but shares numerous similarities with the Morgan sheet. The virtues are again shown (the figure of Justice on the left being most noteworthy in light of Cosimo's deeds), as well as a portrait bust of Cosimo in a niche in the upper story. Each drawing has an equal number of stories with one story open for a painting of Cosimo. The *river gods* found in the Morgan Library drawing are replaced by cherubs in the Pillsbury study. Both drawings have four cherubs bearing torches and two cherubs supporting a medallion.
A comparison of Vasari's drawing for the Borgo Ognissanti (no. D46) with these designs, reflects the continued influence Vasari had on his followers. A survey of all three drawings also emphasizes the influence of Cosimo on the arts and the tribute paid to him and the Medici family in the sixteenth century.

JACOPO ZUCCHI
(Florence 1541-1589/90)

D28. *Study for an Allegorical Figure* (Perhaps the Genius of Architecture)

Pen and brown ink, and brown wash, over a preliminary drawing in black chalk; 7 3/4 x 6 13/16 inches
Lent by Mr. Edmund Pillsbury
Inscription: Annotated in pen and brown ink in an old hand at l.l. *A. Carats*
Provenance: Sir Joshua Reynolds (Lugt 2364); P. Huart ?(Lugt 2084); P. & D. Colnaghi Co., Ltd. (sold 1967)
Exhibitions: Colnaghi, *Old Master Drawings,* June 1967.
This drawing was first attributed to Zucchi by Mr. Philip Pouncey. Zucchi, a member of Vasari's circle, has demonstrated in this drawing, the influential role that the *antique* and Michelangelo played in the sixteenth century. *The Laocoon* group, rediscovered in 1506, had an immediate influence on the Florentines and Romans. The three figures in this composition were inspired by this sculptural group, while the bottom half of the central figure comes from Michelangelo's *Jonah* on the Sistine ceiling.
The drawing also exhibits some of the playful qualities of the Vasari-inspired pen stroke, as well as the growing interest in the 'worm's-eye' view. Evidence of Luca Cambiaso's influence is also suspected by the abstraction of forms into geometric shapes.
Mr. Edmund Pillsbury feels that the drawing was done at the time of the Ruspoli Gallery in ca. 1585.

JACOPO ZUCCHI
(Florence 1541-1589/90)

D29. *The Martyrdom of St. Apollonia*

Pen and ink, brown wash, and white highlights, over black chalk; 9 15/16 x 5 1/16 inches (Circular top)
Lent by Dr. Julius S. Held
Inscriptions: on reverse in pencil, *T. Zuccaro*
Bibliography: *Drawings, The Held Collection,* University Art Gallery, State University of New York at Binghamton, 1970, no. 141, illustrated.
Attributed to Zucchi by Edmund Pillsbury, this drawing is a modello for an unknown altarpiece.

GIORGIO VASARI
(Arezzo 1511-Florence 1574)

D30. *Deposition* (Study for the altarpiece for S. Domenico in Arezzo) c. 1536

Pen and wash drawings; 12 7/8 x 8 3/16 inches
Lent by the Wadsworth Atheneum
Provenance: Purchased from P. & D. Colnaghi & Co., Ltd. London, England in 1951.
Inscriptions: History unknown. However, in J. J. Byam Shaw's hand in pencil on the back of the mount is *Rosso Fiorentino—cp. Volterra Altarpiece, A10841.* Also, on the back of the drawing, written in two places, in what appears to be a modern hand is, *Salviati.*

Exhibitions: The American Federation of Arts, New York, Circulating Exhibition, Nov. 1952-Nov. 1953; Wadsworth Atheneum, Hartford, Conn. *Acquired in Three Years,* 1954; Davidson Art Center, Wesleyan University, Middletown, Conn., *Master Drawings—Symposium on the Graphic Arts,* 1955; Smith College Museum of Art, Northampton, Mass., *Michelangelo's Figura Serpentinata,* 1957, no. 5 in mimeographed cat.; The Detroit Institute of Arts, Detroit, Michigan, *Master Drawings of the Italian Renaissance—A Detroit Adventure in the Arts,* 1960, no. 9, repr. p. 28; The Baltimore Museum of Art, Baltimore, Md., *Bacchiacca and his Friends,* 1961, no. 77, repr. p. 63; Fogg Art Museum, Harvard University, Cambridge, Mass., *Anxiety and Elegance—The Human Figure in Italian Art 1520-1580,* 1962, no. 43; Kent School, Kent, Conn., *Baroque Painting and Sculpture from the Wadsworth Atheneum,* 1966; The School of Fine Arts, The University of Connecticut, Storrs, Conn., *The Figure in Mannerist and Baroque Drawings,* 1967; Vassar College Art Gallery, Poughkeepsie, N. Y., *The Italian Renaissance,* 1968, no. 26.
Bibliography: Bernice F. Davidson, "Vasari's Deposition in Arezzo," *The Art Bulletin,* Sept. 1954, XXXVI, no. 3, pp. 228-231, fig. 2; Reproduced on the cover of *The Evangel,* Christ Church Cathedral, Hartford, Conn., Feb.-March, 1963; Paola Barocchi, *Vasari Pittore,* Milan, 1964, p. 123, no. 2, ill. 2; *Handbook, Wadsworth Atheneum,* Hartford, 1958, ill. p. 31; Karl Frey, *Der literarische Nachlass Giorgio Vasaris,* Munich, 1923, I, p. 79-81. ("G. Vasari in Arezzo on Bartolommeo Rontini in Florenz. 1537 (st. c.) Februar (?)") "Le Ricordanze di Giorgio Vasari," edizioni della Casa Vasari, Arezzo 1929, ed. Alessandro del Vita, pp. 23-24, no. 13.
This is one of the earliest known Vasari drawings. The sheet is a study for the *Deposition,* an altarpiece commissioned by the Compagnia del Corpo di Cristo d'Arezzo in 1536 (Frey I, 77, 79, 80 and *Le Ricordanze di Giorgio Vasari,* pp. 23/24, No. 13).
From this drawing much is learned about the early Vasari. By his own admission, Vasari was a very eclectic artist. He spent countless hours copying and recording the achievements of the antique, the works of the Quattrocento and the works of his contemporaries. We shouldn't be surprised to find that the influence of Rosso Fiorentino and Baccio Bandinelli are evident in this drawing as well as in the altarpiece. Bernice Davidson in her discussion of the two works, calls our attention to the elements that Vasari borrowed from Rosso. The most noteworthy influence is the similarity between Vasari's figure of Christ and the figure of Christ from Rosso's Volterra *Deposition* and Borgo San Sepolcro *Pieta.* Vasari's kneeling Magdalene is based on a female saint in the right side of Rosso's Citta di Castello *Christ in Majesty.* (B. Davidson, "Vasari's Deposition in Arezzo," *The Art Bulletin,* Sept. 1954, XXXVI, p. 230).

It is difficult to discern whether Rosso or Vasari's teacher, Baccio Bandinelli, had a more important influence on Vasari's pen stroke as well as his thin, elongated figures. The system of bold cross-hatching is more characteristic of Bandinelli's drawings, as are the classically structured figures. The facial types of those figures in the lower left may also be a direct influence of Bandinelli.

The *Deposition* was to become one of the preferred motifs in sixteenth century Roman and Florentine painting. The subject was treated by Michelangelo (ca. 1540-1542, plaster cast from lost wax relief; Florence Casa Buonarroti), Daniele da Volterra (1541, Rome, Trinita dei Monti), and Francesco Salviati (c. 1547, Florence Museo di S. Croce).

Including the Rosso and Vasari *Depositions,* all were to share certain stylistic similarities. Each of the artists was interested in the psychological tensions created by the interplay of figures within a shallow space, and around and through the ladders and the cross. Gestures and emotions are abundant as the figures enact the tragedy of the moment.

GIORGIO VASARI (after PERINO DEL VAGA)
(Arezzo 1511-Florence 1574)

D31. *Death of the Martyrs*

Pen and bistre heightened with white on brown paper; 14 5/8 x 13 5/8 inches
Lent by the Fogg Art Museum, Harvard University, Bequest of Charles A. Loeser
Provenance: Charles A. Loeser
Inscription: on the mount in pencil: *Huis le merwede? pres Dordrecht.*
Exhibitions: The John Herron Museum of Art. Indianapolis, Ind., *Pontormo to Greco—The Age of Mannerism,* 1954, no. 1 (as Perino del Vaga); Fogg Art Museum, Harvard University, Cambridge, Mass., *The Anxiety and Elegance, Human Figure in Italian Art* 1520-1580, 1962, no. A6.
Bibliography: Agnes Mongan & Paul Sachs, *Drawings in the Fogg Museum of Art,* Cambridge, Mass., 1946, I, p. 101, II, fig. 101; (see also John Shearman, "Maniera as an Aesthetic Ideal," *The Renaissance and Mannerism: Studies in Western Art,* Acts of the Twentieth International Congress of the History of Art, Princeton, 1963, II, p. 216, repr. XLVIII, no. 7; Otto Benesch, *Master Drawings* in the Albertina, Vienna, 1967, no. 30 for Perino's drawing and its effect on the Florentine artists).
In the 1520's Perino del Vaga excited the Florentines with his drawing for the Church of the Camaldoli. Vasari writes: "Artists and connoisseurs declared they had never seen a more beautiful cartoon, except that designed by Michelangelo for the hall of the council in Florence" (*Lives,* Vol. III, p. 128). Until 1960, the Fogg Art Museum sheet was thought to be the *modello*

for the cartoon that Vasari acclaimed. However, Bernice Davidson in a letter to Agnes Mongan, first questioned the attribution of the drawing to Perino (a suspicion that was supported by Konrad Oberhubner of the Albertina in Vienna in a letter to the former Fogg Art Museum Director, John Coolidge). The original, by Perino, is in the Albertina (no. D31a), while other copies exist in the Louvre (no. 648) and in Chantilly (F.R. 80). The present attribution to Vasari was suggested by Davidson and later supported by Philip Pouncey and Walter Vitzthum. An examination of the two drawings reveals a greater fluidity in the Albertina version. Vasari's copy becomes mechanical; shadows that are subtly treated by Perino become more defined by Vasari, and the copy loses much of the freshness and vitality that excited the Florentines.

In light of Vasari's comments, as well as his youthful practice of copying all that surrounded him, Vasari certainly would not have left this drawing untouched or unrecorded by his own hand if the opportunity had availed itself.

The subject of the drawing is the massacre of the 10,000 martyrs by King Sapor in Persia. The king on the far left, condemns the prisoners to the cross. Some of the semi-clothed prisoners kneel before the king and his staff, straining to free themselves from their bonds. Their fate is seen in the groups of prisoners already condemned and either being led to their execution or meeting death on the crosses.

Like Michelangelo's cartoon, *The Battle of Cascina,* Perino's drawing displays a wide range of forms, costumes, armour, gestures, etc. The material objects, as well as the physical and psychological, made Perino's cartoon an excellent source for the youthful Florentines, Francesco Salviati and Vasari.

GIORGIO VASARI
(Arezzo 1511-Florence 1574)

D32-D33. *Project for A Ceiling*

Pen and brush, brown ink on white paper; 3 7/8 x 8 5/8 inches
Lent by Mr. Janos Scholz
Provenance: Moscardo, Verona
Inscriptions: No. D32, inscriptions on rectangular openings; *capricornus/virgo/aries;* inscription below figures: *FLORA/CERES* No. D33, inscriptions on rectangular openings: *pisces/libra/concer;* inscriptions below figures: *B CCV* (Bacchus)/*VETRVNN*

D34-D35-D36-D37. *Four Planets*

Pen and brown ink (Luna: 3 1/2 x 2 7/16 inches; Sol: 3 5/8 x 2 3/8 inches; Mercury: 3 7/16 x 2 7/16 inches; Chronos: 3 7/16 x 2 3/4 inches)
Lent by Mr. Janos Scholz
Provenance: Moscardo, Verona
Inscription: Each of the figures in the four draw-

ings are identified: D34 *AQUA? MERCURIVS* D35 *AERIS* D36 *LVNA* D37 *SOL*

Bibliography: Walter Vitzthum, *Master Drawings,* IV, no. i, p. 64, repr.

These are two of the seven Vasari drawings acquired by Janos Scholz from the Moscardo Collection in Verona. (Four of the remaining five are also in the exhibition, entitled the *Four Planets,* nos. D34, D35, D36, and D37). Stylistically they are similar to a sheet in the Uffizi (no. 1618 E, no. D34a), and are probably studies for the same project. Barocchi compares the allegories in the Uffizi drawing to the Neapolitan allegories of Monteoliveto. She dates the Uffizi drawing after Vasari's stay in Venice of 1541-1542, suggesting that the Uffizi study may have been a Neapolitan commission, corresponding to an entry in the *Ricordanze* of April 14, 1545. "I remember how on April 14, 1545, Don Pietro Tolledo, Viceroy of Naples, asked me to do for him by the order of Ottaviano de' Medici, who was with the illustrious Duke Cosimo, his son-in-law, who came from Florence, a loggia of worked plaster with figures, ornaments, grotesques, foliage, and colored full of stories worked out in fresco, for the price that it would cost to put the work up, and for the trouble that this would cost to put the work up, and for the trouble that this would cause us, to go from Naples ten miles to Pozzuolo by the sea, we decided that Don Pietro should give us rooms, beds and provisions for the time it would take." (translation from P. Barocchi, *Mostra di Disegni del Vasari e della Sua Cerchia,* 1964, p. 19).

Whether or not the Uffizi drawing was executed for this decoration is questionable. We can be certain, however, that all six of Scholz sheets are either for the same project or one of a very similar nature and of the same period. The figures between the arches, as well as the calligraphy in the Uffizi drawing and the two Scholz drawings are similar.

The *Four Planets, Mercurius, Aeris, Luna,* and *Sol,* were probably intended to occupy a space comparable to the squares between the large squares in the Uffizi drawing.

GIORGIO VASARI
(Arezzo 1511-Florence 1574)

D38. *St. Paul Preaching*

Pen, brown ink, and brown wash, over black chalk; 12 5/8 x 8 3/8 inches
Lent by The Metropolitan Museum of Art, Rogers Fund, 1963
Provenance: Professor J. Issacs, London (sale, Sotheby's, London, March 12, 1963, No. 103: "Giorgio Vasari, Scene from Roman History")
Inscriptions: In pen and brown ink, bottom recto, *DEFENDIT SE CORAM REGE PRESIDE ROM* June 3, 1550 Vasari was commissioned to decorate the Capella del Monte, San Pietro in Montorio, Rome. (*Ricordanze,* p. 66, C, 19 v. 76). Several

of the drawings relating to the vault decoration have been connected with this project (Louvre nos. 2151, 2152 and Uffizi no. 639F.; see Barocchi, *Vasari Pittore,* ills. 40-42). All of the paintings center around the life of St. Paul, Louvre 2151 representing *St. Paul Preaching at Athens, St. Paul Extolling to the Skies* and *St. Paul Conducting before the Pro Council.* Louvre 2152 too is simply a further study for *St. Paul Preaching at Athens.* To this group of drawings should be added the Metropolitan sheet.

The Metropolitan drawing relates very closely to the Louvre drawing (no. 2152). St. Paul in both drawings assumes a similar attitude, the only differences being the position of the Saint's left arm and the positioning of his feet. The Metropolitan sheet is particularly noteworthy for its freshness of concept. The artist is able to instill in his muscular figures an elegance with delicate lines and select areas of ink washes. Vasari's indebtedness to Simone Mosca, a sculptor and architect, who was scheduled to work on the tomb for Cardinal del Monte in San Pietro is evident in the corinthian capitals on the columns flanking the scene.

GIORGIO VASARI
(Arezzo 1511-Florence 1574)

D39. *Ceiling Design for the Sala di Lorenzo il Magnifico, (Il Quartiere di Leone X,, Palazzo Vecchio, Florence)* ca. 1556-62

Pen and brown ink, brown wash, over faint traces of black chalk: the center panel squared in black chalk; 15 1/2 x 14 1/4 inches
Lent by The Pierpont Morgan Library
Provenance: E. Guntrip, Book and Printseller of Tonbridge, Kent; Mr. George H. Fitch, New York City
Inscriptions: By Vasari, below the central panel: *PRESENTE DEL SOLDANO E DALTRI PRINCIPI;* the frames of the blank portrait medallions reading from the top clock-wise: (1) *JULIANUS MED DUX NEMORS* (2) *PETRUS MEDICIS* (3) *IOANNES CARDINALIS DE MEDICIS* (4) *IULIANUS MED PETRI;* the paired virtues reading from the top clock-wise: (1) *AUDACIA* and *BUONEVENTO* (2) *BUON GIUDITIO* and *CLE(M)EN(T)IA* (3) *PIETA* and *FEDE* (4) *FAMIA* and *VIRTU.* The inscription *Geo. Vasari* below the right of the central panel is by a latter hand.
Bibliography: Felice Stampfle, "A Ceiling Design by Vasari," *Master Drawings,* 1968, VI, No. 3, pp. 266-271, pls. 32, 33; Karl Frey, *Der literarische Nachlass Giorgio Vasaris,* Munich, I, 1923, pp. 437-438.

In 1965, Felice Stampfle discovered and identified this drawing. One of the finest Vasari drawings in this country and Europe, the sheet is a preparatory sketch, squared for transfer, for the Sala di Lorenzo il Magnifico (*Il Quartiere di Leone X, Palazzo Vecchio,* no. D39b).

In keeping with the attitude of the decorations of the other rooms of the Palazzo Vecchio, the drawing is the result of a collaborative effort of the artist, Vasari, the humanist, Cosimo Bartoli, and the ancestor, Cosimo. It recalls the deeds of the great 15th century Florentine Lorenzo il Magnifico. In the central square Lorenzo receives offerings from ambassadors representing the King of Naples, the Duke of Milan, the Sultan, the papacy, etc. In the semi-circles surrounding this panel, Lorenzo is depicted seated amongst Florentine scholars and men of letters (left semi-circle). In the top semi-circle we see Lorenzo presiding at the Congress of Cremona; in the right semi-circle he continues the siege of Sarzana, and on the bottom semi-circular opening, we find Lorenzo before the king of Naples, petitioning for peace. Lorenzo is depicted as a humanist, as a scholar, and as a diplomat.

Lorenzo's character is further reinforced by the pairs of virtues that are found in the triangular spaces adjacent to the semi-circles. Portrait medallions, supported by pairs of putti, are also located on the four sides of the drawing.

Stampfle discusses the numerous changes that take place between this drawing and the ceiling. This appears to have been one of the first, if not the first, plan conceived by Bartoli and Vasari. A drawing in the Uffizi (1185 E, no. D39a) is closer in detail to the panel than the Morgan drawing. Stampfle suggests that some of the changes may have been made by Vasari's assistants working from the master design. Vasari's staff, on occasion, deviated from the master's design. However, since the Uffizi drawing is unquestionably by the hand of Vasari it is unlikely that Vasari's students made the changes. The changes were probably made by Vasari following the suggestions of Cosimo I and Bartoli.

A second drawing in the Chatsworth, Devonshire Collection, (Stampfle fig. 4) again falls in line between the Morgan drawing and the panel. The drawing for Lorenzo before the king of Naples has been drastically altered. Full-length figures are replaced by shoulder-head figures; the balustrade is replaced with a balcony crowded with figures. Drawings for other rooms of *Il Quartiere di Leone X* are located in the Cabinet des Dessins at the Louvre, the Gabinetto Disegni e Stampe of the Uffizi, as well as Budapest, Stockholm, and Chatsworth and Ottawa (no. D40).

GIORGIO VASARI
(Arezzo 1511-Florence 1574)

D40. *A Young Soldier in Roman Costume Receiving Tribute from an Old Man Kneeling Before Him* (Study for the Ceiling of the "Sala Cosimo I Granduca" in the *Quartiere di Leone X*, Palazzo Vecchio, Florence) 1559.

Pen and light brown wash on blue paper heightened with white, squared in black chalk; 6 3/8 x 7 3/16 inches.

Lent by The National Gallery of Canada
Provenance: Laemmle; bought from John Manning, London, 1961.
Bibliography: A. E. Popham and K. M. Fenwick, *European Drawings in the Collection of The National Gallery of Canada,* Toronto, 1965, p. 18, no. 23, repr.; *The Manning Gallery 1953-1966,* London, 1966, no. 52, repr. (as Giorgio Vasari); Manning, *Sixteenth Exhibition,* November 1961, no. 80, repr.

Eight paintings decorate the angles of the ceiling of the "Sala of Cosimo I" in the *Quartiere di Leone X* of the Palazzo Vecchio, Florence. This is a finished drawing, squared for transfer for one of the panels. A design for the entire ceiling exists in the Louvre (no. 2174).

Each of the eight paintings in the angles of the ceiling represent towns paying homage to Duke Cosimo I. According to Popham and Fenwick, the section on the Louvre drawing corresponding to this study is inscribed with the word *Borgo*. This presumably would refer to the town of Borgo San Sepolco (*European Drawings in the Collection of the National Gallery of Canada,* 1965, p. 18).

The purpose of the drawing was first identified by Dr. Gunther Thiem. The portion of the ceiling corresponding to this drawing is reproduced in Alfredo Lensi, *Palazzo Vecchio,* Milan, 1929, p. 192.

GIORGIO VASARI
(Arezzo 1511-Florence 1574)

D41. *Seated Man* (Study for the *Arringa di Antonio Giacomini,* Sala Grande, Palazzo Vecchio, Florence) ca. 1563-1566

Black chalk; 11 3/8 x 7 15/16 inches
Lent by the Pierpont Morgan Library
Provenance: Sir Thomas Lawrence; W. Y. Ottley; Colnaghi, London.
Exhibitions: Exhibition 1965, No. 6
Bibliography: Gunther Thiem, "Neuendeckte Zeichnungen Vasaris und Naldinis fuer die Sala Grande des Palazzo Vecchio in Florenz," *Zeitschrift fuer Kunstgeschichte* 1968, pp. 143-150, fig. 4.

This is one of several sketches for the *Arringa di Antonio Giacomini* (no. D12a) in the Sala Grande of the Palazzo Vecchio. It is a study, by Vasari, for the Patricianer, in the left-central foreground, listening with his fellow Florentines to Giacomini's oration, encouraging them to go to war against Pisa.

The drawing joins a rather problematic group of four studies related to the panel. It is the only one that is without question, by the impressario, Giorgio Vasari. It relates closely to Vasari's black chalk studies of this period, particularly to a drawing of Elijah in the British Museum (reproduced in Barocchi *Vasari Pittore,* no. 86). Other drawings from this group, and not by Vasari, are in the Fondazione Horne of Florence and in the

J. B. Speed Art Museum in Louisville (reproduced in Thiem, "Neuentdeckte . . . ," figs. 2 and 5). The third is the drawing from the Scholz Collection (no. D12) which Thiem attributes to Battista Naldini.

It is not surprising to find several artists working on a single panel in the Palazzo Vecchio. It has been demonstrated by Barocchi in her studies, that the decoration of the Sala Grande and the other rooms and halls of the Palazzo Vecchio was accomplished through the efforts of Vasari and his assistants. Vasari was the organizer and, as a consequence, retained control over the project. However, he also permitted certain freedoms to his assistants and it is not surprising to see the hands of Naldini, Cristofano Gherardi, Marco da Faenza, Giovanni Stradanus, Jacopo Zucchi, etc. appearing in the decorations.

GIORGIO VASARI
(Arezzo 1511-Florence 1574)

D42. *Design for a Series of Six Frescoes* (Sala Grande, Palazzo Vecchio, Florence) ca. 1563-1566

Pen and bistre wash; 8 5/8 x 8 1/2 inches (two sheets attached)
Lent by the Fogg Art Museum, Harvard University, Bequest of Charles A. Loeser
Provenance: Charles A. Loeser
Inscriptions: Right sheet, top rectangle: *Papa Alessandro IV da linsegna/ presa di Cascina/ la sacramuccia di Monastero/* middle rectangle: *Edificazione di Fiorenza/ Consiglio della guerra con la deliberazione/ Deliberazione, vigilanza, patienzia fortezza prudenzia/* bottom rectangle: *Carlo IV da privilegi/La presa di vico pisano/ La presa di Casoli*
Left sheet, top rectangle: *PP Leone X da privilegi/La presa de brigantini/* Middle rectangle: *Restaurazione o amplificazione di Fiorenza /Rotta de vinitiani in casentino al b bastione/* Bottom rectangle: *Carlo V* (crossed out) */Batteria del soccorsi fr . . . . Bonbagianni*
Exhibitions: Fogg Art Museum, Cambridge, Mass., *Anxiety and Elegance—The Human Figure in Italian Art* 1520-1580, 1962; The John Herron Museum of Art, Indianapolis, Ind., *Pontormo to Greco—The Age of Mannerism,* 1954, No. 17, repr.
Bibliography: Gunther Theim, "Vasaris Entwuerfe fuer die Gemaelde in der Sala Grande des Palazzo Vecchio zu Florenz," *Zeitschrift fuer Kunstgeschichte,* 1960, II, pp. 97-135, fig. 6; Agnes Mongan-Paul Sachs, *Drawings in the Fogg Museum of Art,* Cambridge, Mass., 1940, No. 197; Paola Barocchi, *Vasari Pittore,* Milan, 1964, p. 58.
In 1566, Giorgio Vasari, with the aid of assistants and advisors, completed the ceiling for the Sala Grande in the Palazzo Vecchio. When the job was completed, thirty-nine panels set in three rows comprised this complete iconographic program. Our complete understanding and appreciation of this staggering achievement is partially realized through the study of these drawings. In 1960, Gunther Thiem reviewed some of the preparations and agonies involved with this project. He published several drawings that lead to an understanding of the project and the most vital sheets were these from the Fogg Art Museum (Thiem, "Vasari's Entwuerfe . . ." pp. 97-135). The drawings are suggestions for six scenes from the history of Florence. Thiem indicates that the six studies belong to the second ceiling plan which is in the Uffizi (no. 7979A) and states that the sheets must be detached and laid end to end (the top of each sheet must meet). The result is an ordering of the drawings as presented to Cosimo I by Vasari.

The scheme, as dictated by the Fogg sheets, was apparently criticized by Cosimo and never reached the final stages. Captions on two of the six drawings are already crossed out on the Fogg Sheet *Carlo V* (bottom left) and *Carlo 4 da privilegi.* The themes of the top two drawings were also dropped in favor of other themes. The middle right sheet, *Edificazione di Fiorenza,* was changed but carried over and the middle left study, *Restaurizione e Amplificazione di Fioreniza,* was not carried through (*ibid.,* p. 104)

These changes were apparently not uncommon to Vasari. Changes were often dictated by Vasari's patron, Cosimo, as well as Cosimo's historical advisor, Don Vincenzo Borghini. Vasari also found his ideas altered on other projects. This may explain studies that are not connected with any project and can only be connected stylistically with other studies.

Other drawings belonging to the second plan are found in the Uffizi (nos. 1490 ORN; 962S; 961S; reproduced in Thiem, figs. 2, 3, 4, 5). Stylistically the sheets are closely related.

GIORGIO VASARI
(Arezzo 1511-Florence 1574)

D43. *Allegory of the Two Parts of Florence* (Study for the Ceiling of the Sala Grande, Palazzo Vecchio, Florence) ca. 1563-1566

Pen and brown ink; 8 1/2 x 10 1/4 inches
Lent by the Art Institute of Chicago, The Leonora Hall Gurley Memorial Collection
Provenance: Dr. William Ogle
Two large tondos terminate the central longitudinal axis of the ceiling of the Sala Grande in the Palazzo Vecchio. This drawing is probably the *schizzo* for one or both of these tondos.
Each of the tondos depicts two districts of Florence and are called *Quartieri di Santo Spirto et Santo Croce* (no. D43a) and *Quarieri di Santa Maria Novella et San Giovanni.* In both panels the dominant figures are the two shield bearers (the *Caporiani*), three cherubs and the lion of the city on the bottom level, the eight cherubs waving banners and seated on a semi-circular concave balcony in the middle level, and the flower strew-

ing figure of Florence (*Fiorenza*) hovering in the top level.

A comparison of the drawing and the tondo reveals the numerous changes made from the earlier idea as represented in the *schizzo*. There are a greater number of figures and the attitudes of the figures are different. However, the arrangement of figures in space has not changed. The relationship of figures to architecture produces the same *horror vacui* as in the tondos.

Gunther Thiem reproduces another drawing from the Ashmolean Museum (Vasaris Entwürfe . . . ," fig. 20) which is a more finished study than the Chicago study. Yet even this drawing exhibits major differences and incompleteness when compared to the tondos.

Copy after GIORGIO VASARI

D44. *Cosimo I with His Artists,* (Sala di Cosimo I de Medici, *Il Quartiere di Leone X,* Palazzo Vecchio, Florence) ca. 1556-62

Pen, brown ink, and wash, heightened with white traces of pink on greenish paper; diameter: 9 1/4 inches
Lent by The Metropolitan Museum of Art, Rogers Fund, 1958
Exhibitions: The Baltimore Museum of Art, Baltimore, Md., *Bacchiacca and His Friends,* 1961, No. 79, repr. p. 70 (exhibited as Giorgio Vasari)
Bibliography: E. Plon, *Benvenuto Cellini,* Paris, 1883. Paola Barocchi, *Vasari Pittore,* Milan, 1964, p. 46; Wolfram Prinz, *Vasaris Sammlung von Kuenstlerbildnissen,* Florence, 1966, p. 15.

This was thought to be a study for the central panel of the Sala di Cosimo I in the Palazzo Vecchio (no. D44a), depicting Cosimo surrounded by his artists. However, Jacob Bean feels that the drawing is an old copy, perhaps after a drawing in the collection of the Castello Sforzesco in Milan. Because of the ruined condition of the Castello Sforzesco drawing, it is impossible to determine whether it is the original or a second old copy after the original design by Vasari.

This drawing, as a copy, is of interest to us because it reveals the changes made from the study to the finished panel. The most notable alteration is in the attitude of Cosimo. In the drawing there is a more distinct relationship between the patron and his artists. Cosimo appears to be talking to the kneeling figure on his left, who has been identified as Niccolo Tribolo. In the painted version he points to Tribolo who now holds a model and stares out of the picture away from all of his artists.

Vasari also reduced the number of artists surrounding Cosimo from twelve in the drawing to ten in the panel. In 1883 E. Plon identified the artists in the finished painting; clockwise from the bottom left foreground; San Marino, Bartolommeo Ammannati, Tasso, Vasari, Baccio Bandinelli, unidentified, Francesco di San Jacopo, Benvenuto Cellini, Tribolo, and Nanni Ungliero, (E. Plon,

Benvenuto Cellini, Paris, 1883). Gertrude Rosenthal has suggested that the unidentified artist be Bacchiacca (Rosenthal, *Bacchicca and His Friends,* 1961, no. 79).

GIORGIO VASARI
(Arezzo 1511-Florence 1574)

D45. *Sacrifice to Jupiter* (?)

Pen, sepia ink and wash on faded white paper; 11 13/16 x 7 7/16 inches.
Lent by the Wadsworth Atheneum
Inscriptions: *Giorgius Vasari* signed l.l. in later hand
Provenance: (Markings on frame of mount: Collector's stamp l.l. of Count Moriz von Fries (1777-1826); *163* in l.l. corner of mat in ink; Lugt No. 2903; 335, white label with black numbers in lower left of mat: cf. drawing of eagles in the Albertina Inv. No. 61 on reverse of Savonarola portrait. One eagle in a similar position.
Exhibitions: The American Federation of Arts, New York, Circulating Exhibition, Nov. 1952-Nov. 1953; The School of Fine Arts, The University of Connecticut, Storrs, Conn., *The Figure in Mannerist and Baroque Drawings,* 1967.
Bibliography: Paola Barocchi, *Vasari Pittore,* Milan, 1964, pp. 136, 44, ill. 57b for copy by Marco da Faenza).

Based on a drawing in the Uffizi (no. D45a), Marco da Faenza, one of Vasari's assistants at the Palazzo Vecchio, is traditionally credited with the invention of this sacrificial scene to Jupiter. However, the discovery of the Wadsworth Atheneum drawing demonstrates that it was the master who first created the image. The Faenza drawing, a copy of the Atheneum sheet, has little of the life exhibited in the Wadsworth Atheneum study. Washes are calculated and belabored and the freedom of Vasari's lines are drawn by Marco with a deliberation and precision that marks the Uffizi drawing as a copy.

The subject of Jupiter is one of the most significant in Roman mythology. Since Jupiter was god of weather, altars were erected on those sites struck by lightning. In this drawing, Vasari has depicted the sacrifice of the lamb to Jupiter. The eagle may be a representation of Jupiter.

GIORGIO VASARI
(Arezzo 1511-Florence 1574)

D46. *Project for an Arch at the Entrance to the Borgo Ognissanti, Florence,* 1565

Pen and brown ink, and brown wash, over a preliminary drawing in black chalk, on a laid paper with a watermark similar to Briquet nos. 1883-4; 16 1/4 x 10 3/4 inches
Lent by Mr. Milton Hebald
Provenance: Sold at Sotheby's, March 25, 1965, lot 61, (as Jacopo Zucchi)
Bibliography: Edmund Pillsbury, "Drawings by Vasari and Vincenzo Borghini for the 'Apparato'

in Florence in 1565," *Master Drawings,* V. 5, no. 3, 1967, pp. 281-283, pls. 24, 25a.

Inscriptions: Recto: upper left *ENTRATA DI BORGO OGNI SANTI N II* (N II is crossed out); inscription on middle right *questo e, il disegno del entra/ta di Borg' ogni Santi/discritto al quad(er) no. 15-16* Verso: below cross-section diagram of the arch *questa e la pianta del arco che e dala banda di la di questo/ medesimo foglio di no 3 disegnato per lentrata di Borg' ogni Sa.*

In 1565 Vasari and Vincenzo Borghini were charged to complete the decorations for the wedding of Francesco de'Medici and Giovanna of Austria. Edmund Pillsbury has demonstrated that this drawing was a study for part of the decorations ("Drawings by Vasari and Vincenzo Borghini for the 'Apparato' in Florence in 1565," *Master Drawings* Vol. V, no. 3, 1967, p. 281-283).

On April 5, 1565, Borghini wrote to Cosimo I in Pisa, sending him nineteen drawings by Vasari and two drawings by himself for the decorations. One sheet described by Borghini in this group of drawings was the Hebald study: " 'I studied the drawings of Borgo Ognissanti, in which, as far as I'm concerned, I would not put the arch, but I would put, in any case, a beautiful and magnificent base, on which I would place a statue of a woman at least 7-8 arms length in height. And these two statues would make a way for passage, leaving enough space, for the passing of a crown, about one and a half to two lengths in diameter, between raised arms, as you can see in the design. Other than the arch, I should not change the concept nor the set-up; however, one must be careful not to complicate the design too much since other things must follow.' " [Num. II. Sequita l'entrata di Borgo Ognissanti, dove, in quanto a me, non vorrei arco, ma disegnerei in sur orgni canto una bella e magnifica base, sopra la quale vorrei una statua di donna il meno di 7 o 8 braccia, e queste due statue si facessero tanto innanzi nella via, che, lasciando lo spazio comodo per il passo, potessero con un braccio in alto aggiungere a tenere l'una dall'un canto, e l'altra dall altro una corona, che arebbe di diametro delle braccia uno e mezzo in due, come nel disegno si vede; e quando pur anche si giudicasse che l'arco vi stesse bene, se ne manda il disegno, e non variera l'invenzione, ne il concetto; ma bisogna anche aver l'occhio di non multiplicar troppo, dico cosi, avendo rispetto a quel che seguira] (*ibid.,* p. 281, note 2, translated).

Even though Borghini liked the drawing, a different scheme was employed.

Arches for such ceremonies were customarily made of wood, painted to imitate marble, and mounted with terra cotta sculpures. The part of the arch shown on this sheet indicates that some surfaces would be decorated with paintings, perhaps scenes in grisaille. At least two statues, probably representing Tuscany and Austria, would

also be included as an integral part of this complex.

The arch, as initially conceived by Vasari, was to have been a splendid setting for this marriage ceremony. Cosimo's sponsorship was to be made evident by the 'imprese' of Cosimo (the turtle with a sail on the base of the arch). But like so many projects of Vasari's during this period, the artist was to alter his plans to conform to the will of others. The final decorations followed Borghini's suggestions.

GIORGIO VASARI
(Arezzo 1511-Florence 1574)

D47. *The Risen Christ, Adored by Saints and Angels, 1568*

Pen and bistre, bistre wash, heightened with white, brown tinted paper; 16 9/16 x 10 1/2 inches

Lent by Mr. Norbert L. H. Roesler

Provenance: Moscardo; Calcellari; House of Savoia-Aosta; Janos Scholz

Exhibitions: The John Herron Museum of Art, Indianapolis, Ind., *Pontormo to Greco—The Age of Mannerism,* 1954, No. 60 (as Benedetto Caliari).

Bibliography: *Le Ricordanze di Giorgio Vasari,* Arezzo 1929, pp. 98/99; Frey, II p. 880; Pluchart, 1889, p. 130; R. Borghini, "Il Riposo," 1584, I, p. 106; Paola Barocchi, *Vasari Pittore,* Milan, 1964, pp. 143/144.

Formerly attributed to Benedetto Caliari, this drawing is one of two studies for the *Resurrection* in Santa Maria Novella, Florence (no. D47a). The altarpiece was painted in 1568 for The First Grand Duke's physician, Andrea Pasquali. The panel was also dedicated to Duke Cosimo. Vasari records: "I remember that at the end of December I put up Andrea Pasquali's panel in Santa Maria Novella, which was 7 arm lengths high, and 4 arm lengths wide; with the resurrection of Christ and four Saints. It cost 200 scudi, but I didn't get more than 150 from him" (translated from the *Ricordanze,* pp. 98/99).

In the drawing we are able to examine Vasari's approach to the painted surface as he works out in detail, lighting, modeling, etc. He employs a painterly approach in the use of wash and highlighting.

The drawing and panel were probably inspired by Agnolo Bronzino's *Resurrection* (no. D46b) painted in 1552 and in S. S. Annunziata, Florence. The position of Christ and the figures at the tomb and Vasari's own admission, suggest that Vasari was conscious of Bronzino's panel while working on the Santa Maria Novella altarpiece.

In 1584, R. Borghini states his puzzlement over the unusual iconography of the altarpiece. The presence of the Apostles at the scene of The Resurrection is contrary to the Holy Scripture. Borghini was bothered because many ignorant people would see the panel. He also criticized the expression of Christ as well as the positions of SS. Damian and Andrew (Barocchi, *Vasari Pittore*, no. 94, pp. 143-144, quotes from Borghini, *Il Riposo*, Firenze, 1584, I, p. 106).

A second drawing related to the altarpiece, attributed to Battista Naldini, is in the Musee Wicar Lille (for reproduction, see Barocchi, *Vasari Pittore*, plate 94).

GIORGIO VASARI
(Arezzo 1511-Florence 1574)

D48. *The Annunciation*, ca. 1571

Pen and brown ink, brown wash, squared in black chalk; Diameter 5 1/4 inches
Lent by The Pierpont Morgan Library
Provenance: Charles Fairfax Murray; purchased by J. Pierpont Morgan in London, 1910
Exhibitions: The Metropolitan Museum of Art, New York, *Drawings from New York Collections —I—The Italian Renaissance*, Nov. 8, 1965-Jan. 9, 1966, no. 104, repr.; The Baltimore Museum of Art, Baltimore, Md., *Bacchiacca and His Friends*, 1961, no. 78.
Bibliography: C. Fairfax Murray, *Drawings by the Old Masters, Collection of J. Pierpont Morgan*, London, 1905-1912, I, no. 35 repr. (as Bronzino); Arthur McComb, *Agnolo Bronzino*, Cambridge, Mass., 1928, p. 152 (not Bronzino); Jacob Bean and Felice Stampfle, *Drawings from New York Collections—I—The Italian Renaissance*, Greenwich, New York Graphic Society, 1965, No. 104, repr.

Although this *modello* has been squared for transfer, scholars have been unable to identify it with any painted composition. Stampfle and Bean correctly dismiss the *Annunciation* in the Louvre as a possibility. It is also clear that the drawing has little to do with the Notre Dame *Annunciation* (no. P17) even though there are elements that are similar in both. The Notre Dame panel dates nearly twenty years earlier than the drawing and was based on an engraving after a lost drawing by Raphael rendered by Marco da Ravenna (no. G2).

Pillsbury has suggested· orally that this drawing may be the cartoon for a lost 'tondo' in the Capella di S. Michele in the Torre Pio in the Vatican which dates in 1571 and is described in Taja's *Description of the Vatican . . . ,"* and in the "Ricordanze" (1929, p. 109).

Evident in Vasari's latter *oeuvre* is an earlier

concept of beauty . . . the beauty or sublime found in earlier Leonardesque drawings and those of Botticelli. This aesthetic which Vasari developed throughout his career, either consciously or unconsciously, is particularly evident in the face of the Virgin. Vasari attains a grace, an elegance of gestures, emotions, etc. in his figures that he worked for in his earlier works and attained shortly before his death. However, wherever Vasari dealt with architectural elements such as the *prie-dieu*, he returned to familiar decorative schemes.

GIORGIO VASARI
(Arezzo 1511-Florence 1574)

D49-D50. *Pair of Allegorical Designs*

Pen and black ink, gray and yellow wash; diameter 3 11/16 inches
Lent by The Metropolitan Museum of Art, Rogers Fund

Vasari's rapid *schizzi* are found in great numbers, and it is likely that many of them remain only as a record of the artist's ideas, never being realized in painted form. These drawings may have been used to complete the iconographic program of a ceiling or a wall. The very nature of the drawings, quick and spontaneous in execution, preclude the possibility that they were finished drawings for a painted surface.

There is no doubt that the drawings belong together. They are two pendants that seemingly depict positive and negative situations. Allegorical design no. D49 pictures a seated, winged female, who holds the head of a seated youth. Overhead three angels (cherubs) are seen flying above the two seated figures. Each of them holds a clay tablet and is showing it to the female who looks up. She appears to be curing the young man with assistance from the flying figures. This leads one to believe that this may be a Biblical scene rather than an allegorical scene. The second design (no. D50) shows a seated figure who seems to be casting a spell over an urn. From a mouth on the urn, water is shown flowing. A dog either sleeping or dead is depicted at the base of the urn. Below the dog, a salamander is shown. Above the kneeling figure a crowd of demonic figures, perhaps devils, in a furious state of mind, fly away from the scene.

Vasari often employed such elements. One is not always certain of the reason for their inclusion and must conclude that they were purely decorative elements and perhaps without any meaning.

D.P.

D1. *Allegory of Peace*   NICCOLÒ DELL 'ABBATE

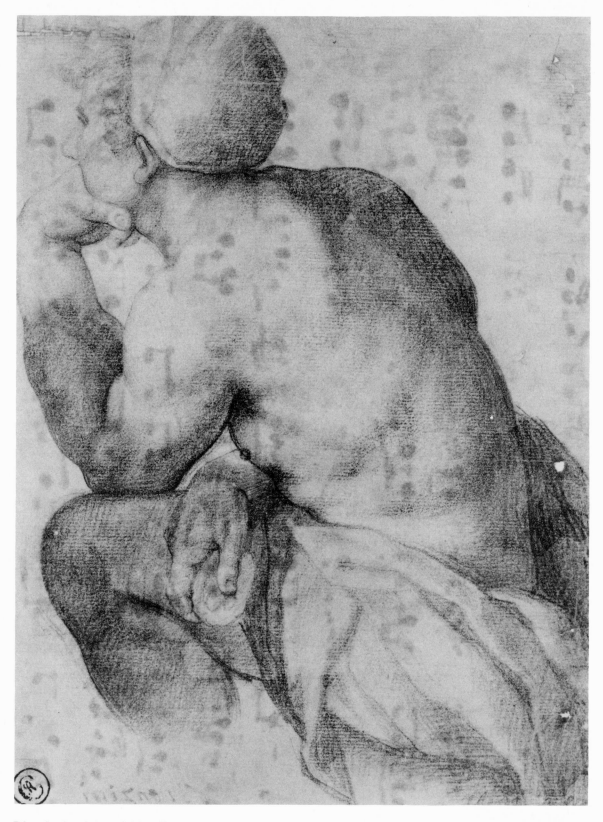

D2. *Study of Seated Male Figure*   ALESSANDRO ALLORI

D2a. *Pearl Divers, Studiolo of Francesco I,*
Palazzo Vecchio, Florence, ca. 1570-1572

ALESSANDRO ALLORI
(Photo: Alinari)

D3. *River God*   BARTOLOMMEO AMMANNATI

D4.　*A Study for a Part of the Mosaic Frieze of
the Siena Cathedral Pavement*　　　　　　　　　　　DOMENICO BECCAFUMI

D5. *The Descent from the Cross*   DOMENICO BECCAFUMI

D6. *Lucretia*　　　　　　　　　　　　　　　GIROLAMO MAZZOLA BEDOLI

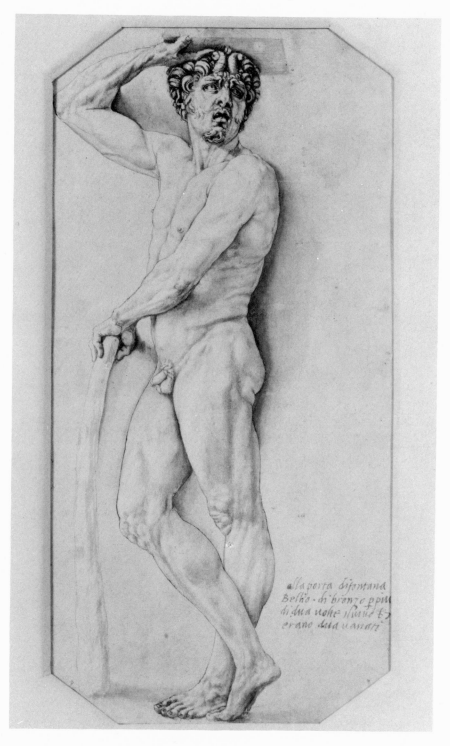

D7. *Standing Nude Male Figure with a Club*   BENVENUTO CELLINI

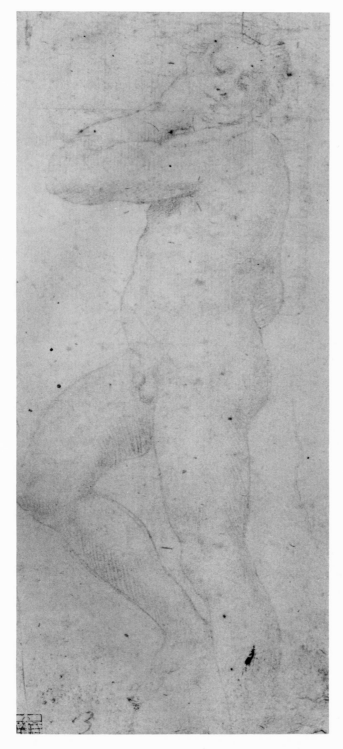

D8. *Standing Youth*　　　　　ROSSO FIORENTINO

D9. *Study for a Ceiling Decoration*   PROSPERO FONTANA

D10. *Thetis Ordering from Vulcan the Armour*   PROSPERO FONTANA
     of Achilles

D11. *Study for the Virgin, St. Agnes, St. Helena,*
       and Other Saints, ca. 1571-1576

GIOVANNI BATTISTA NALDINI

D12. *Project for a Ceiling,* Study for the *Oratory of Antonio Giacomini,* Sala Grande, Palazzo Vecchio

GIOVANNI BATTISTA **NALDINI**

D12a. *Sala dei Cinquecento*
Palazzo Vecchio, Florence

GIORGIO VASARI
(Photo: Alinari)

D13. *Study for the Walk to Emmaus*

LELIO ORSI

D13a. *Walk to Emmaus, London National Gallery*
      (Reproduced with the permission of the London National Gallery)

LELIO ORSI

D14. *Design for a Facade Decoration*   LELIO ORSI

D15. *Three Studies of Putti and of a Seated Boy*

FRANCESCO MAZZOLA
called PARMIGIANINO

D16. *Study for Lucretia*

FRANCESCO MAZZOLA
called PARMIGIANINO

D17. *Bust of a Nude Youth*

JACOPO CARUCCI
called IL PONTORMO

D18. *Manna in the Wilderness*

FRANCESCO MORANDINI
called IL POPPI

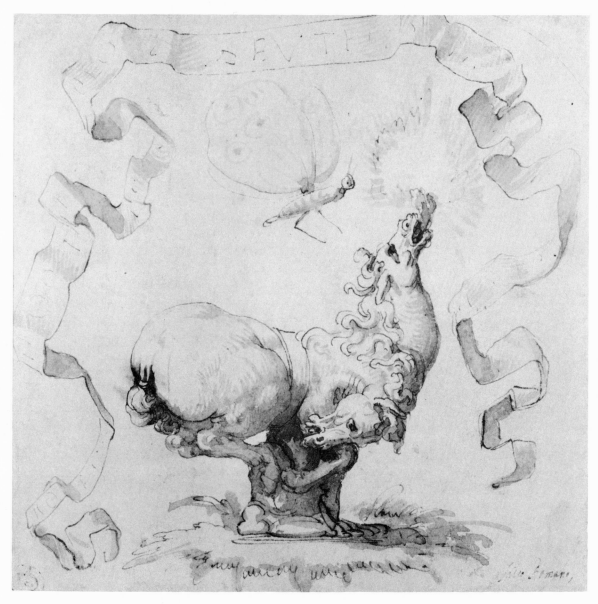

D19. *Design for a Fantastic Emblem*   FRANCESCO SALVIATI

D20. *Warrior Kneeling before an Enthroned Pope*   FRANCESCO SALVIATI

D 20a. *Pope Eugenio IV Commissioning Rannuccio Farnese as the
Military Defender of the Papal States*, Palazzo Farnese, Rome

FRANCESCO SALVIATI
(Photo: Anderson)

D21. *Nobilitas*   STRADANUS

D22. *The Annunciation*   STRADANUS

D23. *Christ Washing the Feet of His Disciples*   STRADANUS

D24. *Scene From the History of Alexander the Great*   PERINO DEL VAGA

TADDEO ZVCHERO
DA S. AGNOLO.
PITTORE.

D25.   *The Sermon of St. John the Baptist* (verso)   TADDEO ZUCCARO

D25. *Kneeling Man* (recto)　　　　　　　　　　　　　　　　TADDEO ZUCCARO

D26. *Design for a Catafalque of Cosimo the Great*   JACOPO ZUCCHI (attributed to)

D27. *Drawing of a Catafalque*   JACOPO ZUCCHI

D28. *Study for an Allegorical Figure* (Perhaps the Genius of Architecture)

JACOPO ZUCCHI

D29. *The Martyrdom of St. Apollonia*   JACOPO ZUCCHI

D30. *Deposition*, Study for the altarpiece for
S.Domenico in Arezzo, c. 1536

GIORGIO VASARI

D31. *Death of the Martyrs*

GIORGIO VASARI (after PERINO DEL VAGA)

D31a. *Martyrdom of the Ten Thousand*
    (Reproduced with the permission of the Albertina, Vienna)

PERINO DEL VAGA

D32. *Project for a Ceiling*   GIORGIO VASARI

D33. *Project for a Ceiling*   GIORGIO VASARI

D32a. *Project for a Ceiling*   GIORGIO VASARI
(Reproduced with the permission of Gabinetto Disegni e Stampe, Uffizi)

D34 *MERCVRIUS (AQVA)*   D35. *AERIS*

D36. *LVNA*   D37. *SOL*

D34-D35-D36-D37. *Four Planets*   GIORGIO VASARI

DEFENDIT SE CORAM REGE ET PRESIDE ROM

D38. *St. Paul Preaching*

GIORGIO VASARI

D39a. *Ceiling Design for the Sala di Lorenzo il
Magnifico, Il Quartiere di Leone X*,
Palazzo Vecchio, Florence, ca. 1556-62
(Reproduced with the permission of Gabinetto
Disegni e Stampe, Uffizi)

GIORGIO VASARI

D39b. *Ceiling for the Sala di Lorenzo il Magnifico,*
Il Quartiere di Leone X, Palazzo Vecchio, Florence

GIORGIO VASARI
(Photo: Alinari)

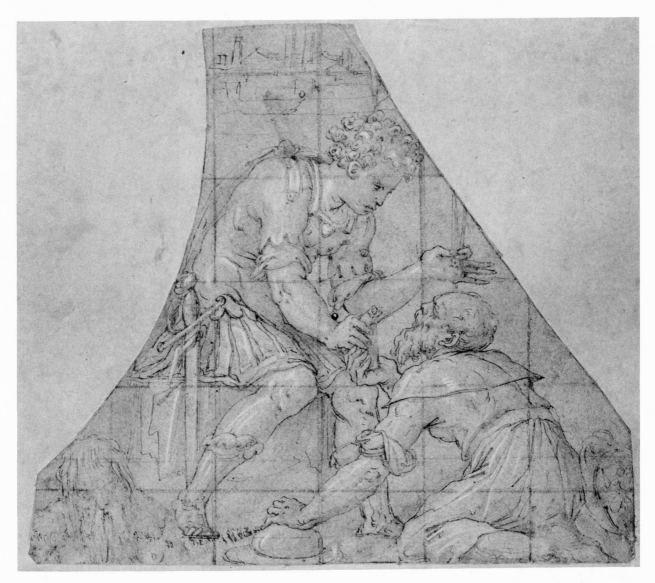

D40. *A Young Soldier in Roman Costume Receiving Tribute from an Old Man Kneeling Before Him* (Study for the Ceiling of the "Sala Cosimo I Granduca" in the *Quartiere di Leone X*, Palazzo Vecchio, Florence) 1559.

GIORGIO VASARI

D41. *Seated Man*, Study for the *Arringa di Antonio Giacomini*, Sala Grande, Palazzo Vecchio, Florence, ca. 1563-1566

GIORGIO VASARI

D42. *Design for a Series of Six Frescoes,* Sala
Grande, Palazzo Vecchio, Florence, ca.
1563-1566

GIORGIO VASARI

D43. *Allegory of the Two Parts of Florence*
Study for the Ceiling of the Sala Grande,
Palazzo Vecchio, Florence, ca. 1563-1566

GIORGIO VASARI

D43a. *Quartieri di Santo Spirito et Santa Croce,*
       Sala Grande, Palazzo Vecchio, Florence

GIORGIO VASARI
(Photo: Alinari)

D44. *Cosimo I with his Artists,* Sala di Cosimo I de'Medici,
Il Quartiere di Leone X, Palazzo Vecchio, Florence,
ca. 1556-62

GIORGIO VASARI,
Copy after

D44a. *Cosimo I with His Artists,* **Sala di Cosimo I**
de'Medici, Il Quartiere di Leone X, Palazzo Vecchio, Florence

GIORGIO VASARI
(Photo: Alinari)

D45. *Sacrifice to Jupiter* (?)

GIORGIO VASARI

D45a. *Sacrificial Scene (Reproduced through the*   MARCO DA FAENZA
       permission of the Gabinetto Disegni e
       Stampe, Uffizi)

D46.   *Project for an Arch at the Entrance to the*
       Borgo Ognissanti, Florence, 1565

GIORGIO VASARI

D47. *The Risen Christ, Adored by Saints and Angels,* 1568

GIORGIO VASARI

D47a. *The Resurrection*
   S. Maria Novella, Florence

GIORGIO VASARI
(Photo Alinari)

D47b. *The Resurrection*
SS. Annunziata, Florence

IL BRONZINO
(Photo Alinari)

D48. *The Annunciation,* ca. 1571   GIORGIO VASARI

Georgio, Vasari.

D49. *Pair of Allegorical Designs*   GIORGIO VASARI

Georgio. Vasari.

D50. *Pair of Allegorical Designs*

GIORGIO VASARI

Graphics

Graphics in the Sixteenth Century

The sixteenth century was the age of the engraver, printer and publisher. The most immediate effect of the popularization of graphics was the dissemination of new ideas, or *invenzioni*. The artistic achievements of Raphael, Michelangelo, Rosso Fiorentino, Parmigianino, and the northern artists were made readily accessible to the Italian artist.

Despite Vasari's account of Albrecht Dürer's engravings and woodcuts, it was this artist that exerted the strongest influence on the Italians at the turn of the century. Vasari describes Dürer (in comparison with Martin Schongauer) as an artist "who displayed more design, better judgment and finer inventions, seeking to imitate life and to approach Italian style which he highly esteemed."[1] He continues his discussion of Dürer stating that the Italians only commended Dürer (and Schongauer) for their diligent engraving.[2] Vasari felt that Dürer would have been the best painter of Italy had he had the advantages of Rome and not the bad models in Germany.[3] Vasari's statements have to be considered in light of his national commitment and obvious prejudices. Even though it was beneath the biographer to credit a non-Italian with great achievements, he occasionally relents to Dürer's greatness.

He credits Dürer with having "fantastic imagination" for the series of St. John on the Patmos and tells us how the Italians copied the animals and monsters.[4] Vasari also records that some of Dürer's copper engravings "amazed the world." Even through Vasari's very clever censorship, Dürer's impact on the Italians is obvious.

Dürer's influence on the Italians, however, did not limit itself to style, technique or *invenzioni*. Dürer made arrangements with Marcantonio Raimondi to publish a series of his copper engravings. Marcantonio, discovering the commercial value of Dürer's prints, copied them on copper with such exactitude, that an enraged Dürer finally appealed to the Venetian Senate to put an end to the unscrupulous act. The problem was resolved when Raimondi was forced to affix his initials to the plates. Raimondi's "practice" introduced to the Italians a commercial practice that would flourish throughout Italy.

Raphael, recognizing the market value of the engraving, not only had Raimondi do engravings of his drawings, panels and frescoes, but also employed his own paint-mixer, Baviera, for print-making. Raimondi did not restrict his activities solely to the works of Raphael and Dürer. His engraving after Titian's *Portrait of Pietro Aretino* was considered by Vasari to be his finest work. Engravings after Michelangelo's *Battle of Cascina* and the works of Baccio Bandinelli were to have an immediate effect on the Italian artist.

Many of the graphic artists following Raimondi were to base their engravings, woodcuts and etchings on the works of the masters. The monumental works of Raphael and Michelangelo, antique sculpture (i.e., the *Laocoön*, no. G3), sarcophagus, gems, and ancient ruins were the subject of the engravers' tools. Images that were often inaccessible or difficult to see were recorded and available to the artist. Michelangelo's *Last Judgment* represented by an engraving in this exhibition by Martino Rota (no. G7).

In this exhibition, we are able to demonstrate how the engraving played a role in one of Vasari's works. Our investigation of Vasari's *Annunciation* (no. P17) re-

---

1. Giorgio Vasari, *The Lives of the Painters, Sculptors and Architects,* New York: J. M. Dent and Sons Ltd., 1963, III, p. 69.

2. *Ibid.,* pp. 69-70.
3. *Ibid.,* pp. 69-70.
4. *Ibid.,* pp 70-71.

vealed certain Raphaelesque elements. After a thorough study of Raphael's surviving works, we were unable to confirm our suspicion of a Raphael influence. However, an engraving after Raphael, attributed to Marco Dente da Ravenna (no. G2), revealed that Vasari borrowed major elements from Raphael. A large segment of the right side of the panel relates closely to the engraving. Vasari either saw the lost drawing or painting by Raphael or based his imagery on the engraving. He mentions the engraving in his *Lives*.

The 16th century experienced innovations in all three major areas of print making. Certainly one must recognize the accomplishments of the engraver. Even while reproducing an existing work, he was developing a personal and distinct style. Hind in comparing Raimondi with Durer, calls the Italian "a genius of limited scope."[5] As an innovator of designs, this is certainly true. He did, however, develop a method that would permit a more direct translation of painting, sculpture, etc. Raimondi cannot be considered a copyist as he often editorialized, introducing new elements and excluding others. His technique, employing lines of strength and sureness, captured the feeling for classical forms. Raimondi's influence on his followers, particularly Agostino Veneziano, Marco Dente da Ravenna and Jacopo Caralgio should also be noticed. Each developed a personal style, exploring the possibilities of the line engraving and refining the medium for artists of greater *invenzioni* such as Domenico Beccafumi (no. G1).

The Italians made the greatest contribution to the technique of the *chiaroscuro* woodcut. Printing with two blocks had been practiced as early as 1506 by Lucas Cranach (*St. Christopher*). However, Ugo da Carpi, an artist of little note, but an experimenter with various techniques in painting and printmaking, added new dimensions to the multiple block woodcut process. Employing three, and as many as four blocks, Ugo was able to produce the line as well as two to three tonal variations (nos. G8 and G9). The crispness of the engraver's line relented to softer images produced by flat areas of color. The resulting effect approaches the effect produced by the watercolor technique.

Parmigianino found the etching process adaptable to the sensitive lines of his drawings. Although his lines were not deeply etched, his experiments paved the way for other Italians of the 16th century, notably Federigo Barocci.

Printing was regarded as a process of reproduction of the master's *disegno*. The purpose of the printer was to exalt the master's creations. The notion of a copy, in a contemporary sense, did not enter their minds. The most immediate result of printing, was the selection, distillation and dissemination of forms. The mannerists owe much to the graphics artists. The print provided them with a visual vocabulary of forms, motifs and gestures that would be repeated in new contexts and decorate the ceilings and walls of Italy's architecture.

D.P.

---

5. Arthur M Hind, *A History of Engraving and Etching*, New York: Dover Publications, Inc., 1963, p. 91.

Selected Bibliography

A. Bartsch, *Le Peintre—Graveur, Vienna* (1803-1821), 21 Vols.
A. M. Hind, *A History of Engraving and Etching*, New York, 1963.
K. Oberhuber, *Die Kunst der Graphik III—Renaissance in Italian 16. Jahrhundert.* Graphische Sammlung Albertina, Vienna, 1966.
J. D. Passavant, *Le Peintre Graveur*, Leipzig (1860-1864), 6 Vols.
Giorgi Vasari, *Le Vite dè piu eccellenti pittori scultori et architetti*, (annotator and comments of Gaetano Milanesi), Florence (1878-1885), 9 Vols.

DOMENICO BECCAFUMI
(Siena ca. 1486-Siena 1551)

G1. *Christ Disputing with the Doctors*

Engraving: 11 5/16 x 8 3/4 inches
Lent by the Lessing Rosenwald Collection
Beccafumi is seldom cited for his capabilities as
a graphic artist. He was an accomplished chiaroscuro woodcut artist and engraver, noted for some
excellent copper engravings. His most noteworthy
copper engravings were a series of scenes dealing
with the profession of the alchemist.

MARCO DENTE DA RAVENNA
(Ravenna, active 1510-?)

G2. *The Annunciation* (after Raphael)

Engraving: 11 3/8 x 10 1/4 inches
Lent by the Art Gallery, University of Notre Dame
Provenance: Richard Ford, 1823, William Sharp;
purchased from P. & D. Colnaghi and Co. Ltd.
1970.
Bibliography: Bartsch XIV, p. 16, no. 15: Colnaghi, *Italian Prints of the Sixteenth Century*,
no. 73, repr.
Marco Dente, called Marco da Ravenna, trained
under Raimondi, and like the older artist, engraved much of Raphael's works. This engraving
has been traditionally attributed to Marco and
it is believed to be after a lost work of Raphael.

MARCO DENTE DA RAVENNA
(Ravenna, active 1510-?)

G3. *Laocoon and His Sons* (after the antique)

Engraving: 19 x 8 15/16 inches
Lent by The Museum of Fine Arts, Boston
Inscriptions: Signed on base to left:
MRCVS.RAVENAS./
On base center: LAOCHOON and. ROMAE.
IN. PALATIO. PONT.IN./.LOCO.
QUI.VVLGO.DICITVR./.BELVIDERE
Bibliography: Bartsch XIV, p. 268, no. 353
In 1506, the discovery of the *Laocoon* group ex-
cited work in all media. This engraving by Marco
Dente, sculptures by Baccio Bandinelli and his
followers, as well as drawings and paintings by
the Romans and Florentines record this important
discovery and illustrate the 16th century interest
in the antique.

GIORGIO GHISI
(Mantua ca. 1520-1582)

G4. *Portrait of Michelangelo*

Engraving: 10 1/2 x 7 3/4 inches
Lent by the Lessing Rosenwald Collection
Inscriptions: "MICHAEL ANGELVS BONAR-

OTA/ TVSCORVM FLOS DELIBATVS/
DVARVM ARTIVM PVLCHERRIMARV/
HVMANAE VITAE VICARIARVM/
PICTVRAE STATVARIAE QVE/ SVO
PENITVS SAECVLO EXTINCTARV/ ALTER
INVENTOR FACIEBAT/ GMF."
Bibliography: *Bartsch* XV, p. 414, no. 71.
Ghisi brought engraving to a new level of so-
phistication in Italy. Although following the
technique of Marcantonio, Ghisi's engravings are
more meticulous than Raimondi's in their rendering. The engravings of Ghisi are characterized by
their fine, more rounded lines and their abundant
use of dots and short strokes. Their tonal values
cover a wide range and the richness of these engravings were seldom surpassed.
Ghisi worked with Luca Penni, Giulio Romano,
Raphael, and Michelangelo. In this engraving,
Ghisi, while optimizing the expressive qualities
and inherent interest of its famous subject also
represents himself as one of the finest engravers
of the sixteenth century.

NICCOLO DELLA CASA
(Lothringen, active in Rome 1543-1547)

G5. *Portrait of Cosimo II de'Medici* (after Baccio Bandinelli), 1544

Engraving: 16 13/16 x 11 1/2 inches
Lent by The Minneapolis Institute of Arts
Inscriptions: Upper left "BACIVS BANDINEL
FLO⁸ 1544;
Upper right "COSMUS/MEDICES/FLORENT/
IAE DVX/.II.
Bibliography: Passavant, VI, p. 124. no 3.
Niccolo is thought to have been a student of
Beatrizet. This engraving was done in 1544 after
a drawing by Baccio Bandinelli. Of particular
interest is the armor 'all'antica' that Cosimo wears.

MARCANTONIO RAIMONDI
(Argine 1470/1480—Bologna 1527)

G6. *Hercules and Antaeus* (after Raphael)

Engraving: 12 7/16 x 8 1/2 inches
Lent by the Lessing Rosenwald Collection
Bibliography: Bartsch XIV, p. 258/9, no. 346.
Raimondi worked under Francesco Francia and
was influenced by Albrecht Dürer. His earliest
known works were after Dürer. In 1510 he
established residency in Rome where he was to
form a working relationship with Raphael that
lasted until the latter's death in 1521. During
this period, Raimondi was to engrave virtually all
of Raphael's works.
Bartsch considers this engraving to be after a
design of Raphael and one of Marcantonio's
better works. (Bartsch, XVI, p. 259, no. 346).
The motif, employed earlier by Mantegna, became a favorite subject of the sixteenth century,
particularly for the sculptor Giovanni da Bologna.

MARTINO ROTA
(Sebenico ca. 1520-Vienna 1583)

G7. *The Last Judgment* (after Michelangelo) 1569

Engraving: 12 1/2 x 9 1/8 inches
Lent by The John and Mable Ringling Museum of Art
Inscriptions: lower left "Mar(tin) vs/Rot(a)/Ben(   )/si Sermo Emanveli Phili/beric Sabavdiae Dvci/.D"
Upper center: "MICHAEL ANGELVS BONAROTVS PATRICIVS PATRICIVS FLORENT.AN.AGENS LXXIII."
Bibliography: Bartsch XVI, p. 260/1, no. 28.
Rota was an engraver and etcher who worked in Venice, Florence, Rome and Vienna. Most of his engravings were after Titian, Zuccaro, Penni and Michelangelo. His technique was influenced by the German engravers, particularly Albrecht Dürer and Cornelis Cort. This sheet after Michelangelo's "Sistine Ceiling" is one of the numerous engravings of the subject done by the Italian engravers.

UGO DA CARPI
(1486-ca. 1532)

G8. *Descent from the Cross* (after Raphael) 1518

Chiaroscuro woodcut in three blocks; 13 9/16 x 10 7/8 inches
Lent by The William Hayes Ackland Memorial Art Center, gift of Dr. W. P. Jacobs
Bibliography: Bartsch, XII, p. 43, no. 22; Le Blanc, II, p. 595, no. 83.
Vasari states that Ugo was the "inventor of engraving on wood in three pieces for showing not only the design but the shadows, half-tints, and lights . . ." ("Vasari on Technique," Translation by Louisa S. Maclehose of the "Introduction to the Three Arts of Design, Architecture Sculpture and Paintings, Prefixed to the Lives of the Most Excellent Painters, Sculptors and Architects," New York, 1960, pp. 281-284 and "Lives," Everyman's Edition, p. 78).
Each of the three blocks was the full size of the print. The initial block would consist of all of the outlines, whereas the second and third blocks would be employed to add shadows and tinted backgrounds. To print the image, the tinted background was forced onto the sheet, followed by the shadows and finally the outlines.
This print was cut in reverse after an engraving by Marcantonio which was after a "Descent from the Cross" by Raphael. The border that bore the inscription "RAPHAEL-VRBINAS" has been trimmed.

Ugo's experiments were carried beyond the medium of the chiaroscuro woodcut. Vasari records Michelangelo's criticism of Ugo's altarpiece for Volto Santo at Rome, which Ugo reportedly painted "with his fingers and other curious tools, not using a brush . . ." "Better if he had used a brush and done it less badly." (*Lives,* III, p. 78).

UGO DA CARPI
(1486-ca. 1532)

G9. *Envy Driven from the Temple of the Muses* (after Balthasar Peruzzi)

Chiaroscuro woodcut; 11 5/8 x 8 7/8 inches
Lent by the Detroit Institute of Arts
Bibliography: Bartsch XII, p. 133, no. 12
Inscriptions: lower left: "BAL.SEN.";
lower right: "PER VGO".
After the design of Peruzzi, Ugo depicts the seated Apollo, surrounded by Minerva and the Muses, ordering Hercules to chase Envy from the Temple of Muses.

ENEA VICO
(Parma ca. 1520-ca. 1570)

G10. *The Studio of Baccio Bandinelli* (after Bandinelli)

Engraving: 12 x 18 7/8 inches
Lent by the Museum of Fine Arts, Boston
Inscriptions: upper right:
"Baccius/Bandi/nellus/invent"
lower left center: "Romae Petrus Paulus Palumbus formis"
Bibliography: Bartsch XV, p. 305/6, no. 49.
Enea Vico's early training was under Barlachi, a mediocre engraver. Vico can be considered as one of Raimondi's huge following. His style varies, reflecting the styles of Jules Bonasone, Agostino Veneziano, Gian Giacomo Caraglio and Marcantonio.
The engraving exhibited here is of particular interest to us as it shows the school of Baccio Bandinelli, as it might have appeared when Vasari studied there as a youth. The engraving, after a design by Bandinelli, shows the master seated to the far right instructing his students. Other students are shown to the left, drawing before a fireplace. The room is filled with plaster models of all descriptions, a disjointed skeleton and huge maps.
Vico was the engraver of several significant prints. Like Rota and Ghisi, he engraved Michelangelo's *Last Judgment.* His engraving of Frans Floris' *Conversion of St. Paul* was to be of particular impact on the "second generation" Mannerists.

G1. *Christ Disputing with the Doctors*   DOMENICO BECCAFUMI

G2. *The Annunciation* MARCO DENTE DA RAVENNA

MICHAEL ANGELVS BONAROT:
TVSCORVM FLOS DELIBATVS
DVARVM ARTIVM PVLCHERRIMARV̄
HVMANÆ VITÆ VICARIARVM
PICTVRÆ STATVARIÆ QVE
SVO PENITVS SÆCVLO EXTINCTARV̄
ALTER INVENTOR FACIEBAT
·G·M·

G4.   *Portrait of Michelangelo*   GIORGIO GHISI

Within the engraving:

COSMVS
MEDICES
FLORENT
IAE DVX
.II.

BAC IVBANO
VINE
FLO. 1544

G5. *Portrait of Cosimo II de'Medici*   NICOLO DELLA CASA

G6. *Hercules and Antaeus*   MARCANTONIO RAIMONDI

G7. *The Last Judgment*

MARTINO ROTA

G8. *Descent from the Cross*   UGO DA CARPI

Literary Sources

GIORGIO VASARI, 1511-1574.
LS1. LE VITE DE PIU ECCELLENTI ARCH-ITETTI, PITTORI, ET SCULTORI ITAL-IANI, DA CIMABUE INSINO A' TEMPI NOSTRI: descritte in lingua Toscana, da Giorgio Vasari Pittore Aretino. Con una sua utile et necessaria introduzzione a le arti loro. In Firenze MDL. [appresso L. Torrentino].
[THE LIVES OF THE MOST EXCELLENT ITALIAN ARCHITECTS, PAINTERS, AND SCULPTORS, FROM CIMABUE TO OUR TIMES, described in the Tuscan language by Giorgio Vasari, Aretine painter; with a useful and necessary introduction by him to their arts. Florence, 1550, 2 v., 994 p.] [publ. L. Torrentino.]
Lent by The Library of Congress
This work was the first attempt to bring together in a narrative form the *oeuvre* of the more important Italian artists from the late thirteenth century to the earlier part of the sixteenth. It opens with a general preface and with separate introductions to the arts of architecture, sculpture, and painting. In these introductions, the origin, materials, and techniques of the art in question are discussed. The work is then divided into three parts. The first part begins with Cimabue, the second with Jacopo della Quercia, and the third with Leonardo da Vinci. A preface dealing with the progress of the arts is inserted at the beginning of each part. Over one hundred and forty artists are individually treated, all of whom were dead by 1550 with the exception of Michelangelo. For the majority, the account includes a list of the artist's masters, a description of his works, mostly with qualitative remarks, a number of anecdotal data pertaining to his life, and an assessment of his position and influence.

GIORGIO VASARI, 1511-1574.
LS2. LE VITE DE' PIU ECCELLENTI PIT-TORI, SCULTORI, ET ARCHITETTORI, scritte, et di nuovo Ampliate da M. Giorgio Vasari Pit. et Archit. Aretino/co' ritratti loro et con le nuove vite dal 1550. insino al 1567 / con Tavole copiosissime de' nomi, dell' opere, e de' luoghi ov' elle sono. In Fiorenza appresso i Giunti 1568.
Lent by The Library of Congress
[THE LIVES OF THE MOST EXCELLENT PAINTERS, SCULPTORS, AND ARCHI-TECTS, written and again amplified by M. Giorgio Vasari, Aretine Painter and Architect / with their portraits and with the new lives from 1550 until 1567 / with detailed indexes of the names, of the works, and of the places where these are [located]. Florence, Giunti, 1568.]
3 v.; v. 1, 529 p., v. 2-3, 1,012 p.
The second edition of the *Lives* varies from the first in a number of ways. In addition to correcting numerous errors, Vasari added much new material, notably about artists still living. He now made use of his collection of drawings by referring to it repeatedly as illustrative material. A woodcut portrait of each artist, individually treated, was also included. This edition has remained the standard one.

GIORGIO VASARI, 1511-1574.
LS3. Autographed letter, signed, dated Florence, January 4, 1558 (1559 in present day chronology), addressed to his patron Cosimo I de' Medici in Poggio a Caiano. After treating miscellaneous matters, Vasari mentions that he has recently completed a first draft of a section of the *Ragionamenti* (see cat. no. LS5).
1 p. (11 9/16 x 8 1/2 inches).
Lent by The Pierpont Morgan Library, Fairfax Murray Collection of European Autographs
Bibliography: Printed in: *Carteggio inedito d'artisti dei secoli XIV, XV, XVI*, ed. G. Gaye, III, (Florence, 1840), p. 10; *Le Opere di Giorgio Vasari*, ed. G. Milanesi, VIII (Florence, 1882), p. 327; *Der literarische Nachlass Giorgio Vasaris*, ed. K. Frey, I (Munich, 1923), pp. 470-72, where the dating of the first part of this letter is contested.

GIORGIO VASARI, 1511-1574.
LS4. Autographed letter, signed, dated Rome January 1, 1571, addressed to the Prince Francesco I de' Medici in Florence. Vasari tells about his work of the past month. He then makes the recommendation (among others) that steps be taken to prevent further damage by rain to his paintings in the Palazzo Vecchio, as had happened in the Sala Grande.
1 p. (10 7/8 x 8 3/8 inches).
Lent by The Pierpont Morgan Library, Fairfax Murray Collection of European Autographs
Bibliography: Printed in: *Carteggio inedito d'artisti dei secoli XIV, XV, XVI*, ed. G. Gaye III (Florence, 1840), pp. 289-90; *Le Opere di Giorgio Vasari*, ed. G. Milanesi, VIII (Florence, 1882), pp. 455-56; *Der literarische Nachlass Giorgio Vasaris*, ed. K. Frey, II (Munich, 1930), pp. 558-59, with annotations.

GIORGIO VASARI, 1511-1574.
LS5. RAGIONAMENTI DEL SIG. CAVALIERE GIORGIO VASARI PITTORE ET ARCHI-TETTO ARETINO. Sopra le inventioni da lui dipinte in Firenze nel Palazzo di loro Altezze Serenissime. Con lo Illustriss. et Eccellentiss. Signor Don Francesco Medici allora Principe di Firenze. Insieme con la inventione della Pittura da lui cominciata nella Cupola. Con due Tavole, una delle cose piu notabili, et l'altra delli huomini Illustri che sono ritratti e nominati in quest'opera. In Firenze. Appresso Filippo Giunti.
MDLXXXVIII.
Lent by The Library of Congress
[DISCUSSIONS OF SIGNOR CAVALIERE GIORGIO VASARI, ARETINE PAINTER AND ARCHITECT, with the most Illustrious and most Excellent Don Francesco Medici, then Prince of Florence, on the "inventions" depicted by him

[Vasari] in Florence in the Palace of their most Serene Highnesses; together with the "invention" of the painting initiated by him in the dome [of the Cathedral]; with two indexes, one of which is of the most notable things, and the other of the illustrious men who are represented and named in this work. Florence, Filippo Giunti, 1588].

1 v., 194 p.

The paintings executed by Vasari and his school in the Palazzo Vecchio in Florence, include scenes of an unusual complexity. Partly in order to facilitate their understanding, and partly to make their content known to a wider public, Vasari wrote a series of imaginary dialogues between the Prince Francesco de' Medici and himself. In these dialogues the Prince is taken from room to room, where the content of each is explained to him in detail. The text concludes with an iconographical description of the dome decoration in the Cathedral of Florence. These dialogues were apparently ready for the press in 1567, but were published only in 1588 by Vasari's nephew, Giorgio Vasari the Younger.

BENEDETTO VARCHI, 1503-1565.
LS6. ORAZIONE FUNERALE DI M. BENEDETTO VARCHI fatta e recitata da lui pubblicamente nell' essequie di Michelagnolo Buonarroti in Firenze, nella Chiesa di San Lorenzo. Indiritta al molto Mag. et Reverendo Monsignore M. Vincenzio Borghini Priore degli Innocenti. In Firenze, appresso i Giunti MDLXIIII.
[FUNERAL ORATION OF M. BENEDETTO VARCHI composed and delivered by him publicly at the memorial service of Michelangelo Buonarroti in Florence, in the church of San Lorenzo; dedicated to the very Magnificent and Reverend Monsignor Vincenzo Borghini, Prior of the Innocenti. Florence, Giunti, 1564].

1 v., 63 p.

Lent by The Library of Congress

The death of Michelangelo was deeply felt by Florentine artists. While arrangements were still being made to have his body transported to Florence, the Academy of *Disegno,* of which Michelangelo had been elected co-head the previous year, agreed to hold for him a lavish memorial service. Benedetto Varchi, a humanist of high reputation, was chosen to deliver the funeral oration. The service took place on July 14, 1564, in the presence of some eighty artists. The oration begins with a detailed account of Michelangelo's career, and ends by showing how his achievements are to be regarded as the culmination of the history of Italian art.

VINCENZO DANTI, 1530-1576.
LS7. IL PRIMO LIBRO DEL TRATTATO DELLE PERFETTE PROPORZIONI DI TUTTE LE COSE CHE IMITARE E RITRARRE SI POSSANO CON L'ARTE DEL DISEGNO / di Vincenzo Danti Perugino all' Illustrissimo et Eccellentissimo Signor Cosimo de Medici Duca di Fiorenza et di Siena. Edizione seconda dopo la rarissima de' Giunti del 1567. Perugia, 1830. [ed. G. B. Vermiglioli]
Lent by The Library of Congress
[THE FIRST BOOK OF THE TREATISE ON THE PERFECT PROPORTIONS OF ALL THE THINGS THAT CAN BE IMITATED AND REPRESENTED WITH THE ART OF *DISEGNO* / by Vincenzo Danti from Perugia [and dedicated] to the most Illustrious and most Excellent Signor Cosimo de' Medici, Duke of Florence and of Siena. Second edition following the very rare Giunti [edition] of 1567. Perugia, 1830.] [ed. G. B. Vermiglioli].

1 v., 96 p.

The concept of harmonious proportion was central to the sixteenth century notion of artistic beauty. While previous writers had stressed the principle of selection or had been primarily concerned with devising fixed arithmetical ratios, Danti, a prominent Florentine sculptor, decided on a different approach. Claiming that it had been Michelangelo's method, he proposed that the determination of proportions should be done first and foremost according to the organic function of each organ. The present *libro,* which was first published in 1567, was meant as the introduction to a work that was to include fifteen books. Only this one appeared.

Maurice Poirier

Ill.mo et Ecc.mo S. mio

Riceuei i Rescritti di V. E. a fauori nella mia lettera Et arrirò dare effetto secondo la commessione di quella; sol resta Et il vescouo di Cortona si ricorda dello spedalingo di Marsilia quanto il Caualier Rosso: impero supplicha in cambio suo Mon S. de Tornabuoni: Et ciò sia prima Et più: la breui cose faro dame: Lo spedalingho de Nocenti mija dato la inclusa et caldamente mela raccomandan' dessiderando Et circha le cose dello spedale quella sappia Et preghi lei Et sara contento per Et in casi di quel Gouerno, no uol fare sensa quel et uolè V. E. alla quale continuo meli raccomande: Io ho finito di far trascriuere il dialogho. delle stanze di sopra. il quale lo condoto cosi abozzato si può dire acagione A V. E possa secondo il suo Giudjio leuarne Et agiugniere: Se V. E. uolè Io comandi aquella intanto Et Io distendo questo delle stanze di sotto un cenno basta. il Giudjio uostro potrò g° basti Di Fiorenze alli iiij di Gennaio MDLVII

D. V. E. Ill.mo

Vmill.mo s.re

Giorgio Vasari

LS3.   Autographed letter from Giorgio Vasari to Cosimo I de'Medici.

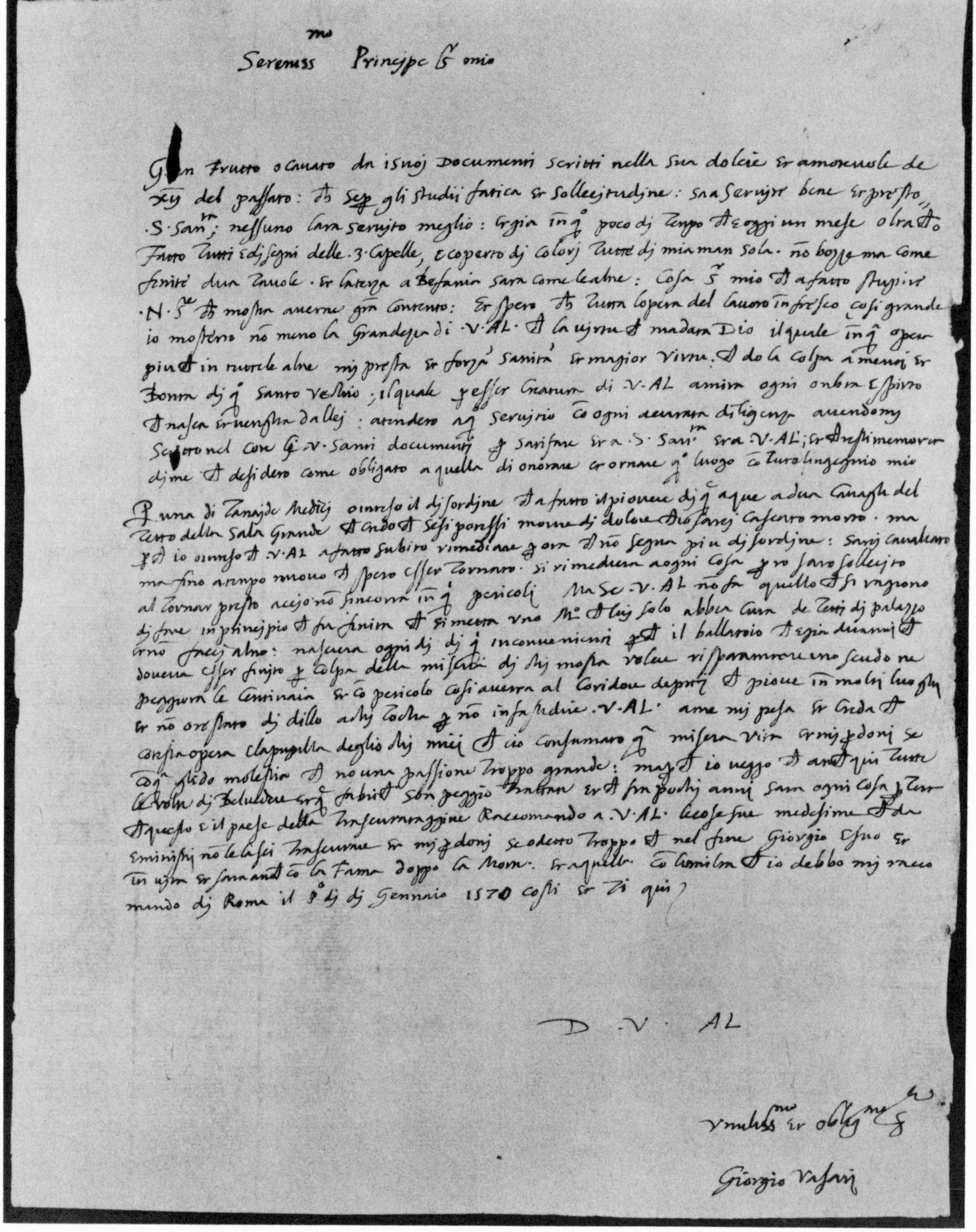

Sculpture

Florentine Sculpture

In the sixteenth century the Florentine sculptors continued the rich tradition of bronze casting which was established by Ghiberti and Donatello. At the opening of the century we have the gigantic personage of Michelangelo whose heroic figures in marble influenced many sculptors. In spite of the fact that we do not have the bronzes by Michelangelo, many of his followers and students used his sketches or models for their work. This early group of sculptors include Zaccaria Zacchi, Pierino da Vinci, Niccolo Tribolo, but probably the most famous was Benvenuto Cellini, who instead of Michelangelo's *terribilita,* so masterly expressed in his large marble figures, turned to smaller compositions in bronze, silver and gold but enhanced them with elegance and grace. Giovanni da Bologna (Giambologna) was the most important Florentine sculptor in the second half of the century and one who represented the Mannerist trends at their best. Preferring Celinni's elegance to Michelangelo's monumentality, Giambologna approached sculpture to be seen from more than one point. His compositions, partially based on Michelangelo's *figura serpentinata,* culminated in his *Rape of the Sabines* (p. 11). The spiraling lines and the great freedom of movements, enhanced by highly polished surfaces, characterize many of his works, and also those which were probably done in his studio. The exhibited works (nos. S2-S14) show clearly this new direction in sculpture.

Selected Bibliography

W. von Bode, *Florentine Sculpture of the Renaissance,* London, 1908.

W. von Bode, *Italian Bronze Statuettes of the Renaissance,* 3 vols., London, 1908-12.

W. von Bode, *Collection of J. Pierpont Morgan: Bronzes of the Renaissance,* 2 vols., Paris, 1910.

Decorative Arts of the Italian Renaissance, exhibition catalogue, Detroit Institute of Arts, 1958-59.

E. Dhanens, *Jean Boulogne,* Brussels, 1956.

Y. Hackenbroch, *Bronzes, other Metalwork and Sculpture in the Irwin Untermyer Collection,* New York, 1962.

H. Keutner, *Sculpture, Renaissance to Rococo,* New York Graphic Society, 1969.

E. Maclagan, *Italian Sculpture of the Renaissance,* Cambridge, 1935.

V. Martinelli, *Scultura Italiana dal Manierismo al Rococo,* Milano, 1968.

J. Pope-Hennessy, *Italian High Renaissance and Baroque Sculpture,* 3 vols., Phaidon, London, 1963.

J. Pope-Hennessy, *Renaissance Bronzes in American Collections,* exhibition catalogue, Smith College Museum of Art, Northampton, Massachusetts, 1964.

J. Pope-Hennessy, *Catalogue of Italian Sculpture in the Victoria and Albert Museum,* Her Majesty's Stationery Office, London, 1964.

L. Planiscig, *Die Bronzeplastiken,* Kunsthistorisches Museum, Wien, 1944.

ANONYMOUS FLORENTINE
16th Century

S1. *Hercules*

Gilded bronze, 8 1/2 inches high
Lent by The Minneapolis Institute of Arts
Provenance: Pulszky, Budapest; Pfungst, London;
J. Pierpont Morgan, New York City; Enrico Caruso, New York City
Exhibitions: Victoria and Albert Museum, London, after 1901, (as a part of the Morgan Collection); The Metropolitan Museum of Art, New York City, 1914; The Baltimore Museum of Art, Baltimore, 1926; *Renaissance Bronzes in American Collections,* Smith College Museum of Art, Northampton, Massachusetts, 1964, illustration no. 2
Bibliography: *Collection of Henry Joseph Pfungst, Esq.,* A descriptive catalogue of a small collection of XV and XVI century bronzes, London, 1901, p. 4, no. 25; *Bronzes of the Renaissance and Subsequent Periods, Collection of J. Pierpont Morgan,* Paris, 1910, Vol. 1, p. VII, no. 11, and p. 4, no. 11, pl. VIII; Dr. Wilhelm von Bode, *Die Italienischen Bronzestatuetten der Renaissance,* Berlin, 1912, Vol. III, p. 16 and pl. CCXXXIII; *Guide to the Loan Exhibition of the J. Pierpont Morgan Collection,* The Metropolitan Museum of Art, New York, 1914, p. 43; Dr. Wilhelm von Bode, *Florentiner Bildhauer der Renaissance,* Berlin, 1921, p. 262; *Catalogue of . . . the Property of the Late Enrico Caruso,* New York, 1923, no. 1004; Dr. Wilhelm von Bode, *Florentine Sculptors of the Renaissance,* New York, 1928, p. 187; A. M. Clark, "Recent Accessions, II," *The Minneapolis Institute of Arts Bulletin,* L1, no. 2 (June 1962), p. 38, illus. p. 41.
This bronze was originally attributed to Bartoldo di Giovanni, a Florentine sculptor (c. 1420-1491) but it is probably a work of a follower who was active in the first half of the sixteenth century.

GIOVANNI DA BOLOGNA
(Douai 1529-Florence 1608)

S2. *Rape of the Sabine Woman*

Bronze, 40 1/2 inches high
Lent by The Metropolitan Museum of Art
Gift of Mr. and Mrs. William B. Jaffe, 1963
Giambologna (Jean Boulogne) began his studies in the workshop of Jacques Dubroeucq of Mons, where he became familiar with the contemporary Italian style. In 1550 Giambologna went to Italy and spent the first two years in Rome. He then moved to Florence, where the Medici became his patrons, and remained there for the rest of his life. In his early works he reveals the combination of the realistic Northern tradition with the Italian idealistic approach. His elegant, elongated figures with smooth surfaces and his works varying in theme and scale had an enormous influence on the sculptors and secured Giambologna the leading role in the second half of the sixteenth century. His famous *Rape of the Sabines,* which was un-

veiled on January 14, 1583 in the Loggia dei Lanzi (see p. 11), was a result of many small bronzes in which Giambologna tried to find the solution for creating a group of three different figures.
There are several versions of this subject and we can assume that most of them were done in the studio with his assistants but probably under Giambologna's close supervision.
For comparison see: E. Dhanens, *Jean Boulogne,* Brussels, 1956, p. 237; also John Pope-Hennessy, *Catalogue of Italian Sculpture in the Victoria and Albert Museum,* London, 1965, p. 468, fig. 489; H. R. Weihrauch, *Die Bildwerke in Bronze und in anderen Metallen,* Munich, 1956, pp. 84-87, no. 110.
Unpublished.

GIOVANNI DA BOLOGNA-ANTONIO SUSINI
(Douai 1529-Florence 1608)

S3. *Rape of the Sabine Woman*

Bronze, 38 1/2 inches high
Lent by Michael Hall Fine Arts Inc.
This version of the *Rape of the Sabine Woman* is two inches shorter than the Metropolitan bronze (no. S2) and there are also some differences in the arrangement of the drapery and in the handling of finished surface; the chiseling is handled in the way in which we find some of the Susini works. Compare the literature given in the previous entry.

GIOVANNI DA BOLOGNA
(Douai 1529-Florence 1608)

S4. *Kneeling Man: A Study for the Rape of the Sabines*

Bronze, 11 3/4 inches high
Signed on base: G. BOLOGNA. F.
Probably dating from c. 1579.
Lent by the Toledo Museum of Art
Gift of Edward Drummond Libbey, 1958
Provenance: Karl Henschel, New York City; Galerie G. Cramer, The Hague
Exhibitions: *Decorative Arts of the Italian Renaissance, 1400-1600,* Detroit Institute of Arts, 1958, cat. no. 272, illustrated; *Renaissance Bronzes in American Collections,* Smith College Museum of Art, Northampton, Mass., 1964, cat. no. 21, illustrated
Bibliography: "Notable Works of Art now on the Market," *The Burlington Magazine,* Vol. 100, 1958, Supplement 3, pl. XII (by error the bronze is said to be mentioned in Dhanens, *Jean Boulogne,* which actually refers to the terracotta in The Metropolitan Museum); "Accessions of American and Canadian Museums," *The Art Quarterly,* Vol. 21, 1958, p. 431, pl. 434.
This figure is probably one of the studies for the lower figure in the large marble of the *Rape of the Sabines* in Florence (p. 11), for which there is also a terracotta in the Metropolitan Museum of Art.

GIOVANNI DA BOLOGNA
(Douai 1529-Florence 1608)

S5. *Hercules and Antaeus*

Bronze, 15 1/2 inches high
Lent by The Virginia Museum of Fine Arts, The
Williams Fund
Provenance: J. and S. Goldschmidt, Frankfurt;
William Salomon, New York City (sale catalogue,
American Art Association, New York, April 4-7,
1923, no. 432, illustrated; Hugo Blumenthal (?)
Bibliography: Elisabeth Dhanens, *Jean Boulogne,
Giovanni Bologne Fiammingo,* Brussels, 1956, pp.
189-198, no. XXXV, fig. 91; Maurice W. Brock-
well, "An Illustrated Foreword: An Explanation
of the Italian Renaissance"; Virginia's Art, "The
Match"; *Art Quarterly,* Vol. XXVI, no. 3,
Autumn, 1963, p. 359; Pinkney Near, "Combat
in the Round", *Arts in Virginia,* Vol. 8, nos. 1-2,
1967-68, pp. 52-55, illustrated.
This bronze could be related to the groups of two
or more figures in which Bologna is exploring the
spiral movement and the vitality of the twisting
figures.

GIOVANNI DA BOLOGNA, Attributed to
(Douai 1529-Florence 1608)

S6. *The Venus from the Fountain in the Boboli
Gardens*

Bronze, 49 inches high
Lent by the Los Angeles County Museum of Art.
The William Randolph Hearst Collection
Provenance: Count G. Stroganoff, Rome; Baron
de Rothschild, Paris; Duveen Brothers, New York
City.
Exhibitions: *Decorative Arts of the Italian Renaissance, 1400-1600,* The Detroit Institute of Arts,
1959, p. 109, no. 273, illustrated; Pomona College, Claremont, California, 1963
Bibliography: W. R. Valentiner, *Gothic and
Renaissance Sculptures,* Los Angeles County Museum, 1951, p. 166, pl. 63.
The present bronze and several versions of small
size were probably cast in the workshop of Giambologna, after the small Fontana della Grotticella
in the Boboli Gardens, behind the Pitti Palace,
Florence, which was executed in marble by Giambologna in 1583.

GIOVANNI DA BOLOGNA
(Douai 1529-Florence 1608)

S7. *Crouching Venus*

Bronze, 9 1/4 inches high
Lent by Mr. Michael Hall
There are several versions of this subject but only
two of them (in the Bargello Museum in Florence
and in the Kunsthistorisches Museum in Vienna)
have been generally accepted as works done by
Giambologna. This bronze, published here for the
first time, certainly reveals the outstanding quality

which might indicate that the finishing work probably was done by the master. The color of the patina
is a warm, rich brown and probably was never
covered with the usual tinted varnish traditionally
used in Bologna's *atelier.*
See: Elisabeth Dhanens, *Jean Boulogne,* Brussels,
1956, p 142, pl. 22, Hans Weihrauch, *Europaische
Bronzestatuetten,* Berlin, 1967, p. 208, p. 251. *Connoisseur,* front cover, August, 1968.

GIOVANNI DA BOLOGNA
(Douai 1529-Florence 1608)

S8. *Bird Catcher*

Bronze, 10 1/4 inches high (including base)
Lent by Mr. Janos Scholz.
There are several similar examples of this title
which probably were done in Giambologna's studio
in association with his assistants. See W. R. Valentiner, "The Bird Catcher by Giovanni Bologna,"
North Carolina Museum of Art Bulletin, II, no. 1,
p. 22, illustrated.

GIOVANNI DA BOLOGNA
(Douai 1529-Florence 1608)

S9. *Figure of a Monkey*

Bronze, 17 1/2 inches high
Lent by Mr. Jack Linsky
Exhibitions: *Decorative Arts of the Italian Renaissance,* Detroit Institute of Arts, November 18,
1958-January 4, 1959, cat. no. p. 110, no. 274,
illustrated.
At the time of the Detroit exhibition (1959) there
was another figure of a monkey on the New York
market. There is also in the Victoria and Albert
Museum in London a head of a monkey but the
head looks upwards. It has been suggested that
the monkey from the Victoria and Albert Museum
was cast for the base of the Fountain of Samson
(see John Pope-Hennesy, *Samson and a Philistine,*
London, 1954, p. 16).

GIOVANNI DA BOLOGNA, Atelier of
(probably by ANTONIO SUSINI)

S10. *Venus Marina (or Fortune)*

Bronze, 21 1/8 inches high
Lent by Michael Hall Fine Arts Inc.
Compositionally the present work is related to
Danese Cattaneo's small bronze statuettes of *Venus
Marina* (Kunsthistorische Museum in Vienna and
the Louvre in Paris) and *Fortune* (Bargello, Florence). However, in contrast to the thick black
patina of Venetian bronzes, the present work has
a golden brown surface, typical of late 16th century Florentine casts. The small sharp angular
folds of the drapery, the squared nails of toes and
and fingers and the working of the hair also point
to Florentine work and in particular suggest Giovanni Bologna's workshop. The present model
appears to be unique.
See also: Leo Planiscig, *Venezianische Bild-*

hauer der Renaissance, Vienna, 1921, pp. 411-415, figs. 432-435; Hans Weihrauch, *Europaischen Bronzestatuetten,* pp. 142-143, figs., 161-162; Hubert Landias, *Les Bronzes Italiens de la Renaissance,* Paris, 1958, p. 116, pl. XXI; John Pope-Henessy, *Italian High Renaissance and Baroque Sculpture,* London, 1963, three volumes, pl. 119.

GIOVANNI DA BOLOGNA, Attributed to
(Douai 1529-Florence 1608)

S11. *Bronze Bull*

Bronze, 9 3/4 inches high
Lent by the Indiana University Museum of Art, Gift of Chancellor Herman B. Wells.
Provenance: Bruschi Collection, Florence.
Bibliography: *Handbook,* Indiana University Museum of Art, 1962, p. 58, no. 136. For other examples see: E. Dhanens, *Jean Boulogne,* Brussels, 1956, pp. 215-216, fig. 197; *Renaissance Bronzes in American Collections,* Smith College Museum of Art, 1964, no. 22, illustrated.
There are several versions of this bronze, two of which are in the United States: one in the Smith College Museum of Art and one in the Drey Galleries, New York City. As with most of the smaller bronzes, perhaps these examples were also the product of Bologna's studio.

GIOVANNI DA BOLOGNA, Attributed to
(Douai 1529-Florence 1608)

S12. *The Bull*

Marble, 13 inches high (with base, 15 1/2 inches high)
Lent by Miss Alice Tully
Provenance: Pietro Tozzi Collection, New York City.
Traditionally this marble bull has been attributed to Bologna but probably is the work of his workshop.

GIOVANNI DA BOLOGNA, Atelier of
Florentine, c. 1600
S13. *Executioner with the Head of St. John the Baptist*
Bronze, 15 5/8 inches high
Lent by Michael Hall Fine Arts Inc.
Several variations of this small bronze sculpture are known to exist. A signed example with a sword, but minus the head, is in the collection of Dr. Erna Wittmann, Budapest. This bronze is called a Mars, as is the example in the Cleveland Museum of Art. Hans Weihrauch, (*Europaische Bronzestatuetten,* 1967, p. 217, pl. 258) says that the later variations in which a severed head is added, transforms the figure into the Executioner of St. John, and are curiosities in the history of unauthorized reproductions, which place the present bronze in the *atelier,* rather than as from the hand of the master himself. Another version, with the head of John the Baptist, is in the Collection of H. Eissler of Vienna.

In 1580, a figure of Hercules slaying the three headed hydra was cast by the goldsmith Giorgio d'Antonio, one of a group of four for the Pitti Palace. There are great similarities between the composition of the Executioner figure and the various bronzes of the Labors of Hercules from Bologna and his workshop, and these figures derive from the marble group of Samson slaying a Phillistine (1567/8) now in the Victoria and Albert Museum, London.

GIOVANNI DA BOLOGNA
(Douai 1529-Florence 1608)

S14. *The Entombment*

Bronze plaque, 10 5/8 x 10 11/16
Lent by Mr. Michael Hall
Bibliography: John Pope-Henessy, *Italian Sculpture in the Victoria and Albert Museum,* London, Her Majesty's Stationery Office, 1964, Vol. 1, p. 476; Vol. III, pl. 498.
In 1588, four bronze reliefs were commissioned by Cardinal Ferdinando de' Medici from Giovanni Bologna for the back of the altar of the church of the Holy Sepulchre in Jerusalem. There is a gilded version in the Victoria and Albert Museum, London, which is considered a later copy. Unlike the present plaque, and the one in Jerusalem, the gilded one included an ornamental design on the front of the sarcophagus, and the striations on the tree trunks above. The handling of the figures appears less free and expressive.
A version of the corresponding relief of the Lamentation over the Dead Christ, from the Jerusalem altar is in the Metropolitan Museum, New York, ("Recent Accessions of European Sculpture," in *Bulletin* M.M.A. n.s. XV, 1956-57, pp. 150-153).

GUGLIELMO DELLA PORTA
(Porlezza c. 1500—Rome 1577)

S15. *The Deposition from the Cross*

Bronze bas-relief, 20 11/16 x 14 3/4 inches
Lent by The University of Michigan Museum of Art
Provenance: John Pierpont Morgan, New York City, ca. 1902; purchased from Duveen Bros., New York City, 1962
Exhibitions: On loan for several years to the South Kensington Museum, London; and to The Metropolitan Museum of Art, New York City, 1913-1916; *Renaissance Bronzes in American Collections,* Smith College Museum of Art, April 9-May 3, 1964, cat. no. 24, illustrated
Bibliography: Antonio Bertolotti, *Artisti Bolognesi, Ferraresi ed Alcuni Altri del gia Stato Pontifico in Roma nei Secoli XV, XVI e XVII,* Bologna, 1885, pp. 205-206; Wilhelm von Bode, *Collection of J. Pierpont Morgan: Bronzes of the Renaissance,* Paris, 1910, Vol. 1, Introduction, p. XXX, Vol. 2, p. 8, pl. XCVI, no. 134, illustrated; Leo Planiscig, *Venezianische Bildhauer der Renaissance,*

Vienna, 1921, pp. 631-634, illustrated, fig. 704; Werner Gramberg, "Guglielmo della Porta," in Thieme-Becker's *Allemeines Iexikon der Bildenden Kunstler,* Leipzig, 1933, Vol. XXVII, pp. 282-283; Ulrich Middeldorf, "Two Wax Reliefs by Guglielmo Della Porta," *The Art Bulletin,* Vol. 17, (March 1935), pp. 90-97; Maria G. Krasceninnikowa, *Guglielmo della Porta,* Rome, 1944, pp. 66-73; Helen Comstock, "The Connoisseur in America," *Connoisseur,* 138 (Sept., 1956), pp. 76, 78; "College Museum Notes, Acquisitions," *The Art Journal,* Vol. XXII, no. 3 (Spring, 1963), p. 172, illustrated, p. 174, fig. 3; "Museum Acquisitions, A Bronze for Michigan," *Apollo,* LXXVII, no. 15 (new series) (May 1963), p. 433, illustrated.

Vasari informs us that Guglielmo was working in 1531 in Genoa in the studio of his uncle Giovanni Giacomo della Porta. In 1537 Guglielmo was in Rome where he was influenced by the works of Perino del Vaga, Michelangelo and Sansovino. Active as an architect, sculptor and the restorer of the antiques, Guglielmo spent most of his life in Rome and Genoa.

There is a drawing in the Duesseldorf Academy, published by Middeldorf (see the Bibliography), which might be compositionally related to this relief.

NICCOLÒ TRIBOLO, attributed to
(Florence 1500-1550)

S16. *Justice*

S17. *Temperance*

Bronze, each 9 inches high
Lent by The Minneapolis Institute of Arts
Provenance: August Zeiss, Berlin
Bibliography: August Zeiss, *Meine Kunstsammlung,* Berlin, 1900, nos. 12-13, pl. 9.

Niccolò studied first in the studio of Giovanni d'Alesso d'Antonio and later with Sansovino. In 1524-25 he was in Rome but a year later went to Bologna where he worked on the portals of San Petronio. Niccolò was called to Florence in 1534 for completion of Michelangelo's Medici Chapel but the work was suspended. Alessandro de Medici employed him for several projects and after Alessandro's death he worked for Cosimo.

M.M.

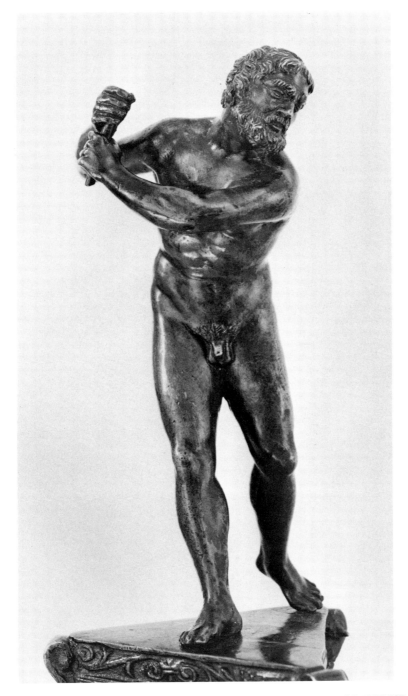

S1. *Hercules*   ANONYMOUS FLORENTINE

S2. *Rape of the Sabines*   GIOVANNI DA BOLOGNA

S3. *Rape of the Sabines*

GIOVANNI DA BOLOGNA - ANTONIO SUSINI

S4. *Kneeling Man* GIOVANNI DA BOLOGNA

S5. *Hercules and Antaeus*

GIOVANNI DA BOLOGNA

S6. *The Venus from the Fountain in the Boboli Gardens*   GIOVANNI DA BOLOGNA, Attributed to

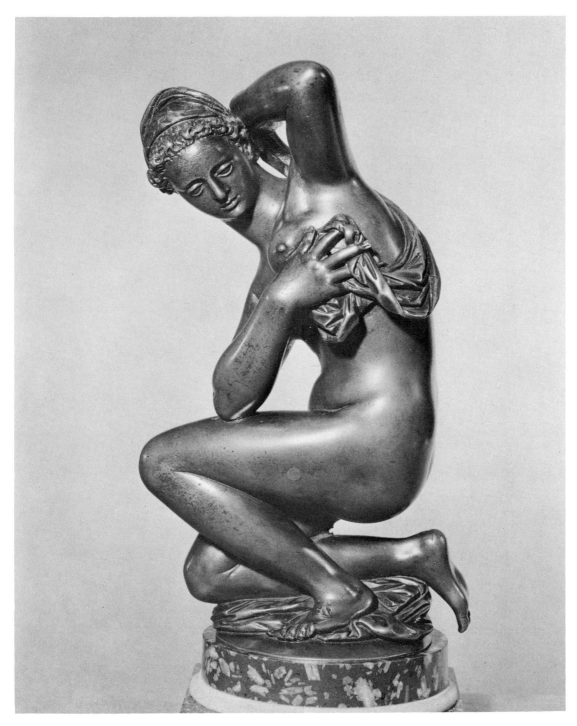

S7. *Crouching Venus*   GIOVANNI DA BOLOGNA

S8. *Bird Catcher* GIOVANNI DA BOLOGNA

S9. *Figure of a Monkey*   GIOVANNI DA BOLOGNA

S10. *Venus Marina*   GIOVANNI DA BOLOGNA, Atelier of

S11. *The Bull*   GIOVANNI DA BOLOGNA, Attributed to

S12. *The Bull*   GIOVANNI DA BOLOGNA, Attributed to

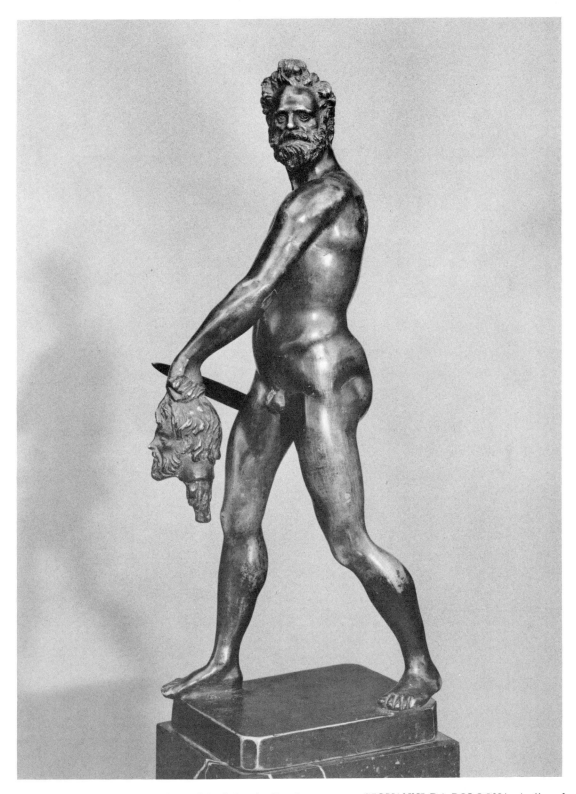

S13. *Executioner with the Head of St. John the Baptist*   GIOVANNI DA BOLOGNA, Atelier of

S14. *The Entombment*   GIOVANNI DA BOLOGNA

S15. *The Deposition from the Cross*   GUGLIELMO DELLA PORTA

S16. *Justice*   NICCOLÒ TRIBOLO, Attributed to

S17. *Temperance*   NICCOLÒ TRIBOLO, Attributed to

Medals

The Mannered Image
Sixteenth Century Medallions

The elegant convulsion which was Mannerism is expressed for us in its commemorative medals. The age of Vasari saw itself as a culmination of the Renaissance; the *weltanshaung* reborn as the Renaissance had now matured. Yet, in the practice of the medallist there are emphatic differences indicative not of a matured worldview but of a worldview evolved almost beyond recognition.

The Renaissance use of the antique medal was as a direct example linking this new age to that of the rediscovered classical age—the medal was valued for its commemorative activity. Hence, the casting of small images was intended as public celebration of public figures; portraits of rulers and military leaders of the quatrocento were crafted for ethical-historical purposes. During the Mannerist period the persona, or public mask, represented on the Renaissance medal is developed into the individual or private person; Renaissance medals affirm general ethical traits with idealized types, while the mannerist medals investigate the subtleties of individual identities.

In 1555 Paolo Giovo illustrated the keen interest which held the minds of his age with the publication of his *Dialogue of Warlike and Amorous Devices*. The search for identity occasioned the practice of including an 'imprese' along with the likeness of the subject. Among the requisites of a device Giovo perceives the need for balancing the expressiveness of both the motto and the design. Further he warns against the device's being either too cryptic or too common; he also suggests that the motto be disguised in a foreign tongue. These admonishments gave rise to a wealth of 'impresi' rooted in allegories (no. *M3*) classical allusions (no. *M18*) and puns (no. *M8*).

Beyond the considerations of sterile history we are confronted with the vitality of the mannerist aesthetic. As artisans grew ever more intimate with the medium of the medallion, a host of structural conceits and stylistic inventions appeared. Relief carving meant problems of proportion and depth (no. *M5*) and circular programs posed questions of play between description and inscription (no. *M1*). Of particular interest here is the well known striking of Charles V by Leoni with its writhing multitude moving in mannered *horror vacui*. The technique which produced these works is also a revealing key; striking (as opposed to casting) comes into vogue in workshops of 16th century Florence, Rome, and Milan. Cellini, for example, talks of his series of decorative punches which allow efficiency in medal production (*Trattato Dell'Oreficeria*); the process of design becomes a convenient vocabulary of form, a concept of technical procedure, which, in this age of *Disegno* relates unmistakably to the use of stock forms and gestures in Cinquecento painting. Vasari's boast: "Where the first masters took six years to paint one picture our masters to-day would only take one year to paint six, as I am firmly convinced both from observation and experience; and many more are now completed than the masters of former days produced" (*Lives* II 154) recalls Benvenuto Cellini's self-assured happiness at turning out a large number of *pile* and *torselli* for Clement VII in one day.

This exhibition of medals attests to a decided move in the 16th century abstracting humanism to a strange flower of individualism expressed through standard forms. The artistic, intellectual, and, often, tragic caprice of the era is amazingly infused in these small but potent commemorative works. In this collection there radiates an insight which, in illuminating both sitter and sculptor, reveals an entire age.

Richard-Raymond Alasko

This part of the exhibition is comprised of selections from the Kress Collection of Renaissance Medals at the National Gallery of Art. These works were authoritatively catalogued by Graham Pollard in a revision of the G. F. Hill Catalogue of Renaissance Medals in the collection of Gustave Dreyfus. The Pollard Catalogue is published by Phaidon Press and printed in London, 1967 for the Samuel H. Kress Foundation. Titles and formal information are taken from the Pollard Work. The legend "K-N" denotes the Kress Collection acquisition number.

FRANCESCO DA SANGALLO
(Florence 1494-1576)

M1. *Giovanni de'Medici Delle Bande Nere,* born 1498, died 1526.

Obv. Bust to right, in cuirass. Around, *IOANNES MEDICES DVX FORTISS*(imus) *MDXXII* Incised on truncation, *FRANC*(iscus) *SAN-GALLIVS FACIEB*(at).
Rev. Winged thunderbolt. Around, *NIHIL HOC FORTIVS*
92mm.   K-N A1051-314A
Giovanni, the father of Cosimo I, the Grand Duke of Florence, was a warrior at heart, rarely staying at home, preferring the craft of the soldier to the scheming diplomacy of his family. His early death occasioned memorial works with more than a common suggestion of bravery. Here, in a medallion made decades later, Sangallo affirms the Florentine respect for the commander's driving spirit.

DOMENICO DE' VETRI
(Florence? after 1480-1547)

M2. *Cosimo I De' Medici,* first Grand Duke; born 1519, Duke of Florence 1537, Grand Duke of Tuscany 1569, died 1574.

Obv. Bust to right, in cuirass. Around, *COSMVS MED*(ices) *II REIP*(ublicae) *FLOR*(entinae) *DVX*
Rev. Capricorn; above, eight stars. Around, *ANIMI CONSCIENTIA ET FIDVCIA FATI*
35 mm. Struck   K-N A1052-315A
Vasari gives a short paragraph to Domenico de' Vetri in the discussion of "Engravers of Cameos and Gems" (*Lives*, VIII, 66) and here he mentions that the artist ". . . also made a portrait of Duke Cosimo the year he was elected by the government of Florence, with the sign of Capricorn on the reverse." Graham Pollard questions the date by the fully bearded image of the 18 year old Cosimo—I hardly find this grounds for argument. Cosimo, son of Giovanni de' Medici Delle Bande Nere and Maria Salviati, was a member of both branches of the Medici; he assumed the title of Duke and the responsibility of Florence from the Florentine Council after the death of Allesandro, with stealth and cunning. His career was that of a crafty and ambitious tyrant, yet his accomplishments raised Tuscany to a prime political and economic power. It is to Cosimo that Vasari dedicated his *Vite*.

FRANCESCO DAL PRATO
(Caravaggio 1512-Florence 1562)

M3. *Alessandro de' Medici,* first Duke of Florence.

Obv. Bust to right, draped. Around, *ALEX-ANDER MED*(ices) *DVX FLORENTIAE I*
Rev. Peace, holding olive-branch, seated to right; with a torch she fires a pile of arms. Around,

FVNDATOR QVIETIS MDXXXIIII Below, sign of Mars.
43mm   K-N A1054-317A
This little medallion is a commendation of Alessandro as harbinger of peace following the siege of Florence in 1530. The personification of Peace found on the reverse bears more than a little resemblance to the much discussed portrait of Alessandro, by Vasari, with its charged emblems.

PASTORINO DE' PASTORINI
(Castelnuovo 1508-Florence 1592)

M4. *Niccolosa,* daughter of Francesco Bacci of Arezzo; wife of Giorgio Vasari the painter.

Obv. Bust to left, hair braided. Around, *NICCO-LOSA BACCI DE VASARI*
Incised on truncation, P1555
Without Reverse. Cast solid.
58 mm. Not an early cast.   K-N A1071-334A
Pastorino is credited with over two hundred medals which he created in the cities of Parma, Ferrara, Novellara, Bologna, and Florence. His early medals (c. 1540-1554) unsigned, contrast with the skillful products of his later works which are, nearly all, signed, dated and which carry a border of large pearls on a raised band. This fine sample of Pastorino's *oeuvre* commemorates Giorgio Vasari's spouse. To her the biographer devotes a laconic mention (1548) in his autobiography: "On completing these works I went that same year to visit the Cardinal de' Monti at Bologna, where he was legate, remaining some days with him. Persuaded by the force of his arguments I decided to take a wife, a thing I had hitherto refused to do, and so espoused a daughter of Francesco Bacci, a noble citizen of Arezzo, as the cardinal wished." (*Lives*, IV, 278)

DOMENICO POGGINI
(Florence 1520 Rome 1590)

M5. *Cosimo de' Medici* (born 1519), Duke of Florence 1537, Grand Duke of Tuscany 1569; died 1574.

Obv. Bust to right, in cuirass and mantle. Around, *COSMVS MED*(ices) *FLOREN*(tiae) *ET SENAR*(um) *DVX II;* below, 1561.
Rev. View of the Uffizi, with the Palazzo Vecchio in the background, in front, Equity with scales and cornucopiae. Around, *PVBLICAE COM-MODITATI*
41 mm. Struck.   K-N A1078-341A
Vasari's office building and artist's workshop which Duke Cosimo I ordered in 1560 is used in this commemorative, striking, example of Cosimo's sense of public responsibility. The figure of Equality (?) announces the new structure which symbolically replaces the *Pallazzo della Signoria* (renamed *Vecchio* 1532) seen in the background. The histrionic renaming of the *Palazzo Signoria* was a method of proclaiming Alessandro Duke of Florence but the new structure by Cosimo stands as an assertion of a different Tuscan rule

shortly to be recognized by Pope Pius V in a Bull proclaiming Cosimo, "Grand Duke" (1569). Poggini, Vasari tells us, "[made] . . . dies for the mint with the medals of Duke Cosimo, and . . . marble statues, imitating as far as possible the distinguished men of the profession." (*Lives*, III, 68) The comparison of the obverse of this medal with the d'Vetri profile (no. M2) shows a suggestively deliberate Cosimo now unmistakably related to his Roman counterparts.

DOMENICO POGGINI
(Florence 1520 Rome 1590)

M6. *Benedetto Varchi*, Florentine historian and man of letters.

Obv. Bust to right, in doublet and cloak. Around, *B*(enedetto) *VARCHI* Incised on truncation, D P
Rev. A man lying at the foot of a laurel-tree; around, *COSI QVAGGIV SI GODE*
Probably the medal mentioned by Annibal Caro in a letter of 20 April 1561, to Leonardo Salviati.
51 mm. Late cast.   K-N A1083-346A
Poggini worked as a medalist for Duke Cosimo and here honors Varchi (also in the Duke's charge) as a contemplative scholar, taking his pleasure beneath the tree of peace (*Cosi Quaggiu Si Gode* "Thus he takes his pleasure here below"). Varchi, funeral orator for Michelangelo, is of particular import to the student of 16th century thought by virtue of his *Due Lezzioni* (published 1549) a mid-century compilation of opinions held by major artists as a comparative discourse of the various arts.

GIOVANNI BERNARDI DA CASTELBOLOGNESE
(b. 1496 d. 1553)

M7. *Clement VII, Pope* (1523-1534).

Obv. Bust to right, bearded, in cape. Around, *CLEM*(ens) *VII PONT*(ifex) *MAX*(imus)
Rev. Joseph revealing himself to his brethren; above *EGO SVM IOSEPH FRATER VESTER*
Modern restrike issued by Vatican Mint.
33 mm. Restrike, from Cracked Dies
                          K-NA1102-365A
"It is without question due to the constant protection of this pope (Clement VII) that Florence and Rome claim the last masterpieces of the Renaissance."[1] Clement, last of the Medici popes, was caught between the conflicting interests of Emperor Charles V, and Francis I. Vasari tells us that Benvenuto Cellini struck two medals of Clement. One of these fine works is reproduced in the Hill catalogue (Plate XVII.I). The likeness is frankly close to that inscribed by Bernardi, included in the present exhibit—it is concerning this medal that Vasari writes of Bernardi: "He had the opportunity of making the portrait of Clement VII by means of the Cardinals Ippolito de' Medici and Giovanni Salviati, with Joseph

declaring himself to his brethren on the reverse. For this His Holiness rewarded him . . ." (*Lives*, III, 61)
The Joseph on the reverse is in similar pose to the Michelangelo Moses. Joseph, St. Augustine states, "was exalted out of the humiliation he endured." (*City of God*, New York, 1950, p. 613 Book XVIII) The reason, it seems, for using a scene of Joseph revealing himself is to connote the sufferings borne by Clement during the siege of Rome.

ALESSANDRO CESATI
(active Rome 1538-1564 Rome?)

M8. *Paul III*, Pope (1534-49)

Obv. Bust to right, in cope. Around, *PAVLVS III PONT*(ifex) *Max*(imus) *An*(no) *XI*
Rev. Ganymede watering the Farnese lilies, resting his left hand on shoulder of the eagle. Above, *OEPNH ZHNOΣ* and, below, *EYPAINEI*
"Oeprn Znros (dowry of Zeus), a pun on the name Farnese, and ev paive (he waters well)" refer to the grant by Paul to his son, Pierluigi, of the Duchies of Parma and Piacenza in 1545.
40 mm. Struck.   K-N A1103-366A
Cesati, called Il Greco, created engravings foremost in grace, perfection and universality . . . so fine in every detail, that it is impossible to imagine better" records Vasari. (*Lives*, III, 66) Paul III was the most energetic of 16th century popes in the beautification of Rome. From him Michelangelo received the commission for the Dome of St. Peter's as well as the order to paint the Sistine *Last Judgment*. The Farnese Pontiff asked Vasari for the frescoes in the great courtroom of the Palace of the Cancelleria. Just as on this coin, we read Cesati's portrait of Paul, with his deliberate features, and on the reverse find the grant of Parma and Piacenza condoned by allusion, so in life, we see Paul as a double-sided coin, who began the important challenge to the Reformation with the Council of Trent, but also engaged in ourageous nepotism and embezzlement.

GIOVANNI ANTONIO DE' ROSSI
(Milan 1517-Rome after 1575)

M9. *Julius III*, Pope (1550-5).

Obv. Bust to left, in cope. Around, [*D*](ivus) *IVLIVS III PONT*(ifex) *O*(P)*T*(imus) *MAX*(imus) *AN*(no) *V*
Without reverse.
Lead, 80 mm.   K-N A1120-383A
Julius III mounted the papal throne with enthusiastic approval as a challenge to the Reformation. His five year reign was something less than spectacular. Vasari speaks kindly of him, particularly insofar as it was from this pope that Vasari received the commission for the Villa Giulia. Julius also gave Palestrina his appointment as Choirmaster at St. Peters.
Giovanni Antonio de' Rossi is principally known

for the cameo of Cosimo I which Vasari sights referring to it as ". . . the work being stupendous, surpassing all his small works . . ." (*Lives*, III, 67) The modeling in this instance could hardly be considered stupendous. It reads as uninspired and, as such, seems a fitting remembrance of the ineffective life of its subject.

GIOVANNI ANTONIO DE' ROSSI
(Milan 1517-Rome after 1575)

M10. *Marcellus* II, Pope (1555).

Obv. MARCELLVS II PONT(ifex) *MAX*(imus). Bust to left, in cope. Below, *IO*(annes) *ANT*(onius) *RVB*(eus) *MEDIOL*(anensis) *Rev.* The Church seated, reading the Gospels, holding a rudder as a symbol of the papal power ruling the world.
76 mm.   K-N A1107-370A
Marcellus, who reigned a short three weeks (10 April-1 May), had time before his death to begin a new life for the papacy. He put off the self-glorifying style of his predecessors and called for reforms which were eventually the triumph of the Counter-Reformation. The composer, Palestrina, was so affected by the astute and sincere pontiff, that he created his memorial mass, *Missa Papas Marcelli,* as tribute to this herald of change.

GIOVANNI ANTONIO DE' ROSSI
(Milan 1517-Rome after 1575)

M11. *PIUS IV,* Pope (1559-1565)

Obv. Bust to left, wearing cope with reclining figure of St. John the Evangelist on orphrey, head of Christ on morse; around, *PIVS IIII PONT*(ifex) *OPT*(imus) *MAX*(imus) *AN*(no) *I* Without reverse.
Another specimen in the British Museum
67 mm.   K-N AII2I-384A
A stern and sober pontiff is celebrated in this sober striking by de' Rossi. It was this pope who recalled the Council of Trent and brought its work to a triumphant finish. With his Bull, *Benedictus Deus,* Pius IV effected the changes too long hoped for, thereby restoring the Church to a position of prestige among both Catholics and Protestants.

GIAN FEDERIGO BONZAGNI
(Parma-d. after 1586)

M12. *PIUS V,* Pope (1566-72)

Obv. Bust to left, in skull-cap and cape with hood. Around, *PIVS V PONT*(ifex) *OPT*(imus) *MAX*(imus) *ANNO VI* and, below, *F*(edericus) *P*(armensis).
Rev. The Battle of Lepanto. On a galley, an angel with cross and chalice; God hurling lightning from above; above, *DEXTERA TVA DOM*(ine) *PERCUVSSIT INIMICVM*
1571
37 mm. Silver, struck.   K-N AIIIO-373A
Michele Ghislieri, a Dominican, set about the task of implementing the Bull, which issued from the Council of Trent. As Pius V, he set into motion improvements in the Church's governance and teachings. He played an active role in politico-religious affairs, excommunicating Queen Elizabeth and releasing her Catholic subjects from obedience to her rule; made contact with the Orthodox church in an attempt to spread the faith in the Orient; and, forming an alliance between Venice, the Papal states and Spain, fought against Islam in the last Christian Crusade, commemorated here by the Battle of Lepanto (1571) in which the forces of Christianity (commanded by Don John of Austria) defeated the Turkish Navy.
Bonzagni, the medallist, was born in Parma and worked in Rome from 1554.

GIOVANNI PALADINO
(Active to ca. 1572)

M13. *Leo X,* Pope (1513-1521)

Obv. Bust to right in cope. Around, *Leo X PONTIFEX MAX*(imus).
Rev. Liberality emptying money from a horn; around her, mitre, cardinal's hat, crown, musical instruments, books, above *LIBERALITAS PONTIFICIA*
One of the modern restrikes issued by the Vatican Mint. Original dies attributed to Paladino.
33 mm. Restrike   K-N A1116-379A
It was in the papacy of Leo X "pastor and father of the peoples . . . happiness proper to an age of gold"* was to be reborn! This confidence is voiced by Aldus Manutius (1445-1515) in his 1513 edition of the works of Plato. Leo was lauded for the sponsorship of scholarly studies of Plato (e.g. founding the Greek Academy in Rome) and in the eye of the 16th century Italian, this son of Lorenzo the Magnificent was easily associated with the rebirth of the Antique Golden Age. Erasmus wrote him: "Leo X, you will give us again the prosperous government of Leo I; the erudite piety and musical taste of Leo II; the fertile eloquence of Leo III . . ."**
This medal is one of a set authored by Giovanni Paladino during the reign of Pius V (1566-1572). Paladino began the series with Martin V (1417-1431), concluding with Pius V.

---

*Quoted in *The Popes as Humanists and Builders,* Page 248.
**Marcel, Raymond, *The Golden Age of the Renaissance,* introduction to the catalog "The Popes as Humanists and Builders," University of St. Thomas, Houston, 1966, Page 47.

LEONE LEONI
(Menaggio 1509-Milan 1590)

M14. *Charles V,* Emperor (born 1500, King of Spain 1516, Emperor 1519-56, died 1558).

Obv. Bust to right, laureate, in cuirass with Fleece and scarf. Around, *IMP*(erator) *CAES*(ar) *CAROLVS V AVG*(ustus).

Rev. Jupiter thundering against the giants. Around *DISCITE IVSTITIAM MONITI* 72 mm. Late cast.   K-N AII63-426A

A commemoration of the 1547 victory of Mühlberg, the reverse celebrates the Emperor as *Deo Optima Maximo* (Jupiter), as he banishes his French and German opposition to Tartarus. Leone, Vasari records, ". . . did a large die for the Emperor's medals, with Jupiter fulminating on the reverse." (*Lives,* IV, 236)

Leoni took every opportunity to demonstrate his virtuosity in this medallion. First, on the obverse, where the laureated Emperor's cuirass becomes an ornamental field serving as background for the order of the Golden Fleece and second, more decorative in its invention and not unlike the Michelangelo's Sistine *Last Judgment,* in its mannerist conceits, the reverse, decidedly assures the viewer of the triumph of the mighty.

LEONE LEONI
(Menaggio 1509-Milan 1590)

M15. *Michelangelo Buonarroti* Florentine artist
(1475-1564)

Obv. Bust to right, in loose cloak. Around, MICHAELANGELVS BONARROTVS FLOR (entinus) AET(atis) S(uae) ANN(o) 88 on truncation, LEO

Rev. A blind man with staff and water-flask, led by a dog. Around, *DOCEBO INIQVOS V*(ias) *T*(uas) *ET IMPII AD TE CONVER*(tentur) 59 mm. A later casting.   K-N AII66-429A

The Milanese sculptor modelled this portrait of the aging Michelangelo in Rome and sent two silver and two bronze examples to him in March of 1561. Vasari tells us . . . "At that time Leoni made a most life-like medal of Michelangelo, and on the reverse, as a compliment to him, a blind man led by a dog, and the legend: *Docebo iniquous vias tuas, et impii ad te convertentur.*" (*Lives,* IV, 165). The verse from Psalm 51; 13 "Then I will teach transgressors thy ways, and sinners shall be converted unto thee" was suggested by Michaelangelo and thus identifies him as the blind beggar. Federigo Zucchari made a drawing of Michelangelo in the same pose while at the Piazza Mattei in 1547. (John Pope-Hennessy, *The Portrait in the Renaissance,* New York, 1966, p. 209)

Leoni's portrait on the obverse is curtly and precisely modelled, the edges of the garment clear and deliberate, the structure of the handsomely held head, emphatically chiseled.

LEONE LEONI
(Menaggio 1509-Milan 1590)

M16. *Baccio Bandinelli,* Florentine sculptor
(1493-1560)

Obv. Bust to right; around, *BACIVS BAN-*(dinellus) *SCVLP*(tor) *FLO*(rentinus)
Rev. Within a laurel-wreath, *CHANDOR ILLESIS*

The original was struck, and showed on the

truncation of the arm LEO, which is not apparent on this specimen.
39 mm.   K-N AII65-428A

A competent remembrance of a little loved man, this medal by Leoni portrays the bitter characteristics of the sculptor eulogized by Vasari as an artist who, ". . . always spoke ill of the works of others, no one could endure him, and all who could do so returned his abuse with interest. He made abominable accusations in the courts, and these were retorted upon him. He was always engaged in litigation, and seemed to delight in it. But his designing was so excellent that it obscures all his other defects, it was the thing to which he devoted his chief energies, and it wins him a place among the best artists." (*Lives,* III, 215) This medallion, candidly modelled, aided by Leoni's decorative skill, possesses sparse charm.

LEONE LEONI
(Menaggio 1509-Milan 1590)

M17. *Andrea Doria,* The Genoese Admiral born
1468; died 1560, and the *Artist*

Obv. Bust of Doria to right, in cuirass and cloak; behind shoulder, trident; around, *ANDREAS DORIA P*(ater) *P*(atriae)
Rev. Bust of Leoni to right; behind, a galley and a fetter-lock; below, anchor at end of chain attached to the galley. All in a circle of fetters.
43. mm. Struck; original might come from dies
K-N AII67-430A
1541

A famous token of gratitude, this medal is meant to witness the thanks of Leoni for his release from the galleys by Doria in 1540. Leoni had been accused of a plot on the life of the papal jeweler Pellegrino de Leuti. The suggestion of the Neptune theme is not original with the artist, rather it appears in works by Bronzino, Bandinelli and others who synchronized the mythic characteristics of the Sea God with the legendary magnitude of Andrea Doria.

ANONYMOUS ITALIAN
16TH CENTURY

M18. *Pietro Bacci* called Aretino, the satirist
(1492-1557)

Obv. Bust to left, wearing gown and chain. Around, *DIVVS PETRVS ARETINVS*
Rev. Truth, nude, seated, crowned by Victory; before her, a Satyr crouching, she points at him and looks up at Jupiter(?) in the clouds. Around, *VERITAS ODIUM PARIT*
60mm.   K-N AII64-427A

If one would know the age of Vasari, one must have an equal knowledge of the caustic and clever Aretino. This critic, who held the dying father of Cosimo I (Giovanni de' Medici delle Bande Nere), befriended major artists and indirectly aided the foster child of Mannerism, the School of Fontainebleau, is depicted here in a fashionable but not impressive design. This portrait lacks the verve and purposefulness of the well known oils which express the poet's incisive wit.

M1. *Giovanni de'Medici Delle Bande Nere,*   FRANCESCO DA SANGALLO
   born 1498, died 1526.

M2. *Cosimo I de' Medici,* first Grand Duke   DOMENICO DE' VETRI

M3. *Alessandro de' Medici,* first Duke of Florence.   FRANCESCO DAL PRATO

M4. *Nicolosa,* daughter of Francesco Bacci of Arezzo; wife of Giorgio Vasari

PASTORINO DE' PASTORINI

M5. *Cosimo de' Medici* (born 1519), Duke of Florence 1537, Grand Duke of Tuscany 1569; died 1574.

DOMENICO POGGINI

M6. *Benedetto Varchi*, Florentine historian and man of letters.

DOMENICO POGGINI

M7. *Clement VII, Pope* (1523-1534).

GIOVANNI BERNARDI DA CASTELBOLOGNESE

M8. *Paul III,* Pope (1534-49)

ALESSANDRO CESATI

M9. *Julius III,* Pope (1550-5).   GIOVANNI ANTONIO DE' ROSSI

M10. *Marcellus* II, Pope (1555).   GIOVANNI ANTONIO DE' ROSSI

M11. *PIUS IV*, Pope (1559-1565)   GIOVANNI ANTONIO DE' ROSSI

M12. *PIUS V*, Pope (1566-72)   GIAN FEDERIGO BONZAGNI

M13. *Leo X*, Pope (1513-1521)   GIOVANNI PALADINO

M14. *Charles V*, Emperor (born 1500, King of   LEONE LEONI
        Spain 1516, Emperor 1519-56, died 1558).

M15. *Michelangelo Buonarroti* Florentine artist
(1475-1564)

LEONE LEONI

M16. *BACCIO BANDINELLI,* Florentine
sculptor born 1493; died 1560

LEONE LEONI

M17. *Andrea Doria,* The Genoese Admiral born
1468; died 1560, and the *Artist*

LEONE LEONI

M18. *Pietro Bacci* called Aretino, the satirist
born 1492; died 1557

UNATTRIBUTED ITALIAN 16TH CENTURY